DREAM AND FANTASY IN CHILD ANALYSIS

DREAM AND FANTASY IN CHILD ANALYSIS

Edited by

Samy Teicher and Michael Günter

KARNAC

First published in English in 2015 by
Karnac Books Ltd
118 Finchley Road, London NW3 5HT

Copyright © 2015 to Samy Teicher and Michael Günter for the edited collection and to the individual authors for their contributions.

The rights of the contributors to be identified as the authors of this work have been asserted in accordance with §§ 77 and 78 of the Copyright Design and Patents Act 1988.

All rights reserved. No part of this publication may be reproduced, stored in a retrieval system, or transmitted, in any form or by any means, electronic, mechanical, photocopying, recording, or otherwise, without the prior written permission of the publisher.

British Library Cataloguing in Publication Data

A C.I.P. for this book is available from the British Library

ISBN 978 1 78049 191 2

Edited, designed and produced by The Studio Publishing Services Ltd
www.publishingservicesuk.co.uk
e-mail: studio@publishingservicesuk.co.uk

Printed in Great Britain

www.karnacbooks.com

CONTENTS

ABOUT THE EDITORS AND CONTRIBUTORS — vii

INTRODUCTION — xi
On children's dreams—a brief introduction
by Samy Teicher and Michael Günter

CHAPTER ONE
Children's dreams—where the wild things are — 1
  Elisabeth Brainin

CHAPTER TWO
The development of children's dreams — 23
  Veronica Mächtlinger

CHAPTER THREE
A child is playing, a child is dreaming — 39
  Florence Guignard

CHAPTER FOUR
On not being able to dream: the role of maternal containment in the therapy of a young child who suffered from night terrors   55
Christine Anzieu-Premmereur

CHAPTER FIVE
Dream, phantasy, and children's play: Spaces in which a child approaches thinking between wish-fulfilment, mental processing of affect, and mastering of reality   69
Michael Günter

CHAPTER SIX
On reflection in dreams or "Do people get lost if they go up in a hot air balloon?"   93
Daniel Barth

CHAPTER SEVEN
Dreams and narratives in the developmental process: Dreaming as perceived in developmental psychology and neurobiology   111
Kai von Klitzing

INDEX   125

ABOUT THE EDITORS AND CONTRIBUTORS

Christine Anzieu-Premmereur teaches at the New York Psychoanalytic Institute and at the Columbia University Center for Psychoanalytic Training and Research. Both there and at the New York Psychoanalytic Institute she is director of the Parent–Infant Psychotherapy Training Program. She is a member of the Societé Psychanalytique de Paris and of the Association for Psycho-analytic Medicine, and is Assistant Professor in Psychiatry at Columbia University, New York. She is also a member of the American Psychoanalytic Association and of the IPA. In addition, she is chair of the study group for Parent–Infant programs in psychoanalytic institutes of the American Psychoanalytic Association. In private practice, she works as an adult and child analyst, and also gives parent–infant counselling. Among others, she has been published in French on play in child psychotherapy and on psychoanalytic interventions in parent–infant treatment. She has written several articles in journals and has also contributed to books on mother-hood, maternal functions, and child development.

Daniel Barth, MD, is consultant for child and adolescent psychiatry and psychotherapy; is an adult, adolescent, and child psychoanalyst;

and is a member of the Swiss Association for Psychoanalysis (SGPsa/IPA). He was a visiting researcher from 1995 to 1996 at the Anna-Freud Center with Mary Target, and was a member of a psychoanalytic reading group led by Peter Fonagy from 1995 to 2000. Together with Michael Günter and Kai von Klitzing he edited the journal *Kinderanalyse*. His main focus is on using the analytic setting for psychoanalytic work on early disorders with child, adolescent, and adult patients.

Elisabeth Brainin, MD, lives and works in Vienna. She is a psychiatrist, psychoanalyst, child analyst in private practice, and a training analyst with the WPV/IPA. Until 2002 she was the medical director of the Child Guidance Clinics in Vienna. She has contributed to publications on child analysis, trauma, anti-Semitism, history of psychoanalysis, and the after-effects of persecution. She is on the editorial board of the journal *Kinderanalyse* and is a member of SEPEA.

Florence Guignard was born in Geneva and started her analytic training at the Swiss Society for Psychoanalysis. In 1970 she moved to Paris. In 1979 she became a member and in 1982 a training analyst at the Paris Psychoanalytic Society. She founded two associations for child analysis, the French APE (1983) and the European SEPEA (1993). At present she is responsible for training in child analysis at SEPEA. From its inception she has been a member of the IPA Committee on Child and Adolescent Psychoanalysis (COCAP) and has held the chair since 2009. She was the editor responsible for the publication of *L'Année Psychanalytique Internationale* (an annual French publication in book form of the International Journal of Psychoanalysis) and remains a member of the editorial board. She has given numerous lectures and further training courses in Europe, South America, and Canada, has published more than 250 articles in various journals and volumes of collected papers in several languages, and has written three monographs: *Au Vif de l'Infantile* (1996), *Épitre à l'Objet* (1997)—both of which have been translated into Italian, Spanish, Portuguese, and Turkish—and *La relation mère/fille. Entre partage et clivage* (2001).

Professor Michael Günter, MD, was born in 1957, and studied medicine, history of art, and empirical cultural studies in Tübingen and Vienna. He is a consultant in child and adolescent psychiatry and psychotherapy, psychosomatic medicine, and is a psychoanalyst for adults, children, and adolescents. He is a training analyst for DPV/IPA, and is the medical director of the Clinic for Child and Adolescent Psychiatry and Psychotherapy at the Stuttgart Clinical Centre. Together with Kai von Klitzing and Daniel Barth, he is editor of the journal *Kinderanalyse*. He has written and edited several books and numerous articles. His main focuses of work include: adolescence, psychoanalytical social work, forensic child and adolescent psychiatry, child and adolescent psychosomatics.

Veronica Mächtlinger has recently retired. She is a Child and Adult Analyst who formerly worked in private practice in Berlin, where she was also an active member and training and supervising analyst in the Berliner Institut (Karl-Abraham-Institut). She trained as a Child Analyst in London under Anna Freud, at the former Hampstead Clinic (now the Anna Freud Centre).

Samy Teicher has a diploma in psychology and is a psychoanalyst and child psychoanalyst, member of the Vienna Psychoanalytic Society (WPV/IPA), training analyst for psychoanalytic psychotherapy (WPA/WPV) and a training group analyst (ÖAGG—Austrian Study Group on Group Therapy) with coaching and supervision in private practice in Vienna. He has contributed to publications on trauma and its after-effects, child analysis, anti- Semitism, and the history of psychoanalysis.

Professor Kai von Klitzing, MD, is director of the University Clinic for Child and Adolescent Psychiatry, Psychotherapy, and Psychosomatics in Leipzig, and chair of Child and Adolescent Psychiatry at the University of Leipzig. He is a psychoanalyst for children, adolescents, and adults, a member of the Swiss Society for Psychoanalysis, and training analyst in the German Psychoanalytic Association (DPV/IPA). Together with Michael Günter and Daniel Barth he is editor of the journal *Kinderanalyse*. He is also a co-editor of the journal *Infant Mental Health*, and is president elect of the World Association for Infant Mental Health (WAIMH). His main scientific interests are in developmental psychopathology, depressions and anxiety disorders in childhood and adolescence, early parent–child relationships, and psychotherapy research. He has contributed to publications in German, English, and French including, among others, books on psychological problems in immigrant children, psychotherapy in early childhood, psychoanalysis in childhood and adolescence, and reactive attachment disorders.

INTRODUCTION

On children's dreams—a brief introduction

Samy Teicher and Michael Günter

> We are such stuff as dreams are made on, and our little life is rounded with a sleep. (Prospero in Shakespeare's *The Tempest*, 1610–1611)
>
> The dreams we are in search of occur in children. They are short, clear, coherent, easy to understand and unambiguous; but they are nevertheless undoubtedly dreams. You must not suppose, however, that all children's dreams are of this kind. Dream-distortion sets in very early in childhood. (Freud, 1916–1917, p. 126)

Is attention to dreams experiencing a renaissance? With reference to the modern psychoanalytical understanding of dreaming one is tempted to agree. Bion's concept of the human psyche—as a mental apparatus that dreams day and night and in doing so transforms raw sensory data and emotions into (dream) thoughts—has stimulated fresh interest in dreams in psychoanalytical literature. The reverie of the analyst, this dream-like thinking, allows him or her to capture the unconscious exchange between analyst and analysand. And even more, dreaming is the very prototype of symbolic thinking, in that it metabolises the unthinkable (β-elements) to create a first form of thinking in images and pictograms. In order to acquire meaning, the things we perceive and experience have to be dreamt. In children there is a particularly close connection, as described above, between their dreams when asleep and their dreamlike thinking while awake, their play, and their imaginative life. Nevertheless, psychoanalytical discussion has focused mainly on the dreams of adults, and dream activity in childhood has been largely ignored.

The contributions to this book, containing talks given at the Conference in Vienna on "Dream and Fantasy in Child and Adolescent Psychoanalysis and Psychotherapy", focus on this close connection between children's imaginative world, their dream life, and play. Is it a dream that a child is recounting or is it rather a fantasy to be regarded as equivalent to a dream? Children's play, too, presents important material that allows us to draw inferences about the subconscious. Indeed, dreams, daydreams, fantasies, and play were originally treated as of equal importance in child analysis.

How do child analysts work with dreams at the practical and theoretical levels? In the practice of child analysis today do we find analysis of dreams and the classic differentiations between manifest and latent content? Is attention accorded to the mechanisms of condensation, displacement, and so on, described by Freud?

An English study (Lempen & Midgeley, 2006) observed that child analysts show widely divergent approaches to children's dreams. Left to themselves children rarely recount their dreams. They are only moved to do so when specifically asked by someone. Young psychoanalysts in the early days of their practice after qualifying tend to hold back here and it is only after a few years experience that they actively invite the children to recount dreams.

The current discussion on working with children's dreams and their equivalents in today's practice of child psychoanalysis forms the central focus of the contributions collected in this book.

Vienna saw the emergence of Sigmund Freud's psychoanalysis and the publication of a modern interpretation of dreams, and it is in these writings that we find the first comments on children's dreams. It was also Vienna in the 1920s and 1930s that was home to two of the pioneers of child analysis, Hermine Hug-Hellmuth and Anna Freud, the third being Melanie Klein in Berlin.

Every school of psychoanalysis has felt indebted to Freud's *Interpretation of Dreams*, which in his view "remained what is most characteristic and peculiar about the young science" (Freud, 1933a, p. 7), but in the treatment of children and adolescents the interpretation of dreams has more and more retreated into the background.

Elisabeth Brainin (Vienna) demonstrates how children's dreams can be understood in terms of their ego development. She describes the development of wish dream to anxiety dream according to Anna Freud's developmental lines. She also sees the development of dreamwork as being parallel to ego development and illustrates this with dreams from the various stages of development in children and adolescents.

Veronica Mächtlinger (Berlin) develops a vivid picture of working with dreams in child analysis and of its theory, basing this on accounts of several classic psychoanalytic cases—among others Little Hans (Freud, 1909b) and the case of Johnny (Niederland, 1957). She illuminates the importance of the analysis of children's dreams and the degree to which it has played a part in the development of child analysis and child psychotherapy. Dreams allow us an insight into the increasingly complex inner life of children as they grow, and point to the psychical importance we should attribute to them. She sees dream as a "compromise formation seeking a regressive solution for Oedipal conflicts and castration anxieties". Her very detailed account underlines the great importance of dreams in the analytical treatment of children.

Florence Guignard (Paris) examines the dream activity of two- to six-year-old children. In this phase of development, secondary processes and defence mechanisms are not as yet fully structured. Play is seen as equivalent to dreaming in small children, just as is phantasy—as we indeed expressed it in the title of our conference. In eight vignettes she describes various aspects of dreaming. Play as an equivalent to dreaming was already mentioned. In the section on dreaming to daydreaming, she shows with the example of the "capacity of reverie" what compromise solutions between adult and infantile forms of thinking in the mother are needed to find the "right communication level with the kind of psychic functioning" of her child. To access children's dreams, Guignard examines the children's verbal fantasies and activities in drawing and playing.

Of their own accord children will not recount their dreams. Both child analysts and child therapists commonly report this and it is true and yet also untrue, since fantasies or drawings can be regarded as equivalent to dreams and so be treated as if they were dreams. We also know from clinical experience that children ought to be asked about their dreams, even if the difference between a dream and a fantasy is not clear. Christine Anzieu-Premmereur, for instance, asks a child if he has had "bad dreams", as every child does have them, and she always receives an answer. Children also have "good dreams" that they are happy to relate—but they have to be asked.

From a French-American point of view Christine Anzieu-Premmereur (New York) describes how, in the course of the treatment of a child who was unable to dream and was suffering from a massive trauma, the first dream then emerged and enabled the child to express inner sensations, tensions, and conflicts symbolically and verbally. The dreams help the analyst and the small patient to understand the process of controlling its drives. The ability to dream and to form representations from dreams depends on an ability to regulate and symbolise emotions.

In his contribution Michael Günter (Tübingen) first of all draws on two dreams recounted in "The earliest dream of a young child" by Niederland (1957) to show that a processing of thoughts and affects can already be demonstrated in the dreams of very young children. He goes on to observe that, in terms of structure, children's fantasies and play amply fulfil the function in analysis of adult dreams: in play—as Winnicott writes—children invest dream meaning and feeling into external objects. Play allows the child not only to enact and express its inner life, it also creates a space for thinking and action with the aid of which the child can grasp and digest the associated affects. Günter illustrates this in two case studies of traumatised children.

Daniel Barth (Basel) explores the question of reflection in dreams. In colloquial language, reflecting on thinking means thinking about thinking, referring to a person's ability to think about his inner thoughts. As psychoanalysts we call this the capacity for introspection. Barth however sees his contribution as "thoughts about what the beginnings of thinking might look like". "Thinking is an experimental kind of acting", as Freud wrote. Barth hypothesises that dreaming is a precondition for thinking. The dream thought is not translated into motor activity because, if it were, the dream would end and the dreamer would wake up. "So dreaming can be seen as a kind of mental action in a trial form." He elaborates this argument with a clinical vignette.

Focusing on a different aspect, Kai von Klitzing (Leipzig) examines the contribution of neuroscience to the theory of dreams, and elucidates certain preconditions for dreaming from the neuroscientific and the psychoanalytical viewpoints. He describes in a clinical example the development of a transition from a dream-like narrative in the therapeutic sessions to the narration of dreams, in which the libidinally charged activities of infantile sexuality become visible.

We are grateful to Harriet Hasenclever for providing the translation of the successive chapters in the book, with sensitivity for the nuances of expressions in the originals and understanding of the differing theoretical psychoanalytical perspectives collected here. We should also like to express our thanks to Karnac Books Ltd, and in particular to Mr Rod Tweedy, for enabling us to present this book to an English-speaking readership.

> The whole day I kept my secret to myself; it was the dream I had had the night before. It was an uncanny one. I was visited by a ghost. (Walter Benjamin, 1991)

References

Benjamin, W. (1991). *Gesammelte Schriften VI: Fragmente vermischten Inhalts*. Frankfurt am Main: Autobiographische Schriften, Suhrkamp.

Freud, S. (1909b). *Analysis of a Phobia in a Five-year-old Boy*. S. E., 10: 1–150. London: Hogarth.

Freud, S. (1916–1917). *Introductory Lectures on Psycho-analysis*. S. E., 15–16: 1–240, 241–463. London: Hogarth.

Freud, S. (1933a). *New Introductory Lectures on Psychoanalysis*. S. E., 22: 1–182.

Lempen, O., & Midgley, N. (2006). Exploring the role of children's dreams in psychoanalytic practice today. *Psychoanalytic Study of the Child, 61*: 228–253.

Niederland, W. G. (1957). The earliest dreams of a young child. *Psychoanalytic Study of the Child, 12*: 190–208.

Shakespeare, W. (1610–1611). *The Tempest*, Act 4, Scene 1.

CHAPTER ONE

Children's dreams—where the wild things are

Elisabeth Brainin

My title, with its reference to Maurice Sendak's book (1963), indicates the content of children's dreams. These present us with an intricate interweaving of drive wishes and anxieties, fears of being deprived of love, castration anxiety, fears of bodily mutilation, and aggressive impulses.

In Sendak's children's book this is depicted in a playful and imaginative way, which is why the book appeals to children. Aggression, identification with his parents, the wish to be big and powerful, and all oral needs make their appearance in the pictures and text of the book.

I shall give a brief account of the content of the book—the illustrations cannot unfortunately be reproduced here although they express the dream nature of the story particularly well. They can, however, be assumed to be well-known. The mother gets very cross with Max, calling him a wild thing and he shouts back at her with the words "I'll eat you up!" Aggressive though this sounds, eating someone up can be interpreted as a concealed declaration of love.

The motif reappears later in his dream. The residue of the day that Max processes in his dream would be his mother's words "wild thing" and his answer "I'll eat you up". Max sails off into the wide, wide world, sailing far away and for a long time, and finally reaches the place where the Wild Things are, and they are even wilder than he is, terrifying, noisy, and clearly not tame. But Max is stronger than they are, he can even tame them because he looks them straight in the eye without blinking. Max's mother could not tame him, he still went on being wild and did not listen to her. The mother's words find their way into the dream and take shape in the wild things he meets. There is not only one wild thing but many, and they make Max their king and set up a real, wild rumpus.

This represents the wish in the dream: Max's wish is to be the strongest, to be wilder than all others, king of wild things, and set up a wild rumpus. However, he then sends the wild things off to bed without their supper—so here he is putting himself in the place of his mother! In this we see the reversal of passive into active: what he has "suffered" he now inflicts on the wild things. But then he sinks into sadness and the fear of being alone. He longs for home, particularly when he smells the good food, and this smell finally wakes him.

His hunger can be seen as a somatic stimulus, the smell of the food as a sensory stimulus with both of them acting as a stimulus to the dream. Max no longer wishes to be king, he is not afraid of the wild things ("We'll eat you up, we love you so"). He leaves them and sets off home, and when he wakes up in his room he can smell his supper ("and it was still hot").

His hunger, the smell of food, and the longing for his mother are stronger than the dream and finally make him wake up. Oral needs linked to the mother, aggression, fantasies of omnipotence, and desire for autonomy all find their place in Max's dream. We can also find further features of dream-work: residues of the day are found in distortion, reversal of passive into active, condensation, and symbolisation. Sendak uses all these elements in his story. The wish to be wild, wicked, powerful, and voracious is restricted to the dream. The developing superego is recognisable at the end of the dream: when Max wakes up he is himself and safely at home with real prospects of instinctual drive fulfilment.

Ego development and dreamwork

I shall not go into detail here on the psychoanalytical theories of the origins of dreaming. I wish rather to focus my comments on one particular aspect that we can trace in children's dreams: the development of the ego observable in their dreams at different ages.

The development of a child's ego is paralleled by the development of dreamwork and its mechanisms—which I shall go into in detail in a later section. And equally the dreams themselves undergo development. The path from wish dream to anxiety dream that Freud depicted in *The Interpretation of Dreams* (Freud, 1900a) can almost be termed a developmental line, in the sense of the developmental lines Anna Freud described for instinctual drives. (A. Freud, 1965a). The earliest instinctual drive wishes undergo psychical processing because they inevitably cause conflicts. The frustration over unsatisfied oral wishes in infants is the basis of the first wish dreams and these offer hallucinatory satisfaction. When the hallucinatory drive fulfilment can no longer be maintained the infant wakes up.

I shall not go into Freud's descriptions of the earliest wish dreams of children in *The Interpretation of Dreams* as they are sufficiently well-known. I would simply like to choose two children's dreams from his work "On dreams" (Freud, 1901a).

The first dream: a little girl of one and half years old has vomited because she had apparently got an upset stomach eating strawberries. She is not allowed to eat anything for a day and at night she is heard saying her own name in her sleep and adding "Stwawberries, wild stwawberries, omblet, pudden!", she was thus dreaming of eating a meal, and she laid special stress in her menu on the particular delicacy of which, as she had reason to expect, she would only be allowed scanty quantities in the near future (p. 643). The dream is attributed to his daughter Anna.

The second dream: Hermann, nearly two years old, is given a basket of cherries and he is only allowed to eat a few of them. On the next day he announces cheerfully "Hermann eaten all the chewwies!" (p. 644)

Both these dreams are completely clear, they are pure wish dreams. These are dreams in which the latent and the manifest dream content are as yet indistinguishable from one another since the wish appears in the dream without disguise.

Later in ego development what happens in the dream is influenced by conflicts with the emerging superego and also by traumatic situations that the child has experienced during the day, and that have involved separation fears, object loss anxiety, or castration anxiety. It can also be the anticipation of a danger or the repetition of traumatic experiences that result in anxiety dreams and in the typical sleep disorders of children of this age.

Sleep disorders in the child's second year of life are seen by Selma Fraiberg (1950) as derived from the first major conflicts in anal development in a child's life. She believes the conflicts develop from the child's desire to soil and the resulting fear of love deprivation. One could also say it is a question of the wish both to enjoy retaining the faeces and to enjoy excreting, and the resulting fear of love deprivation. This produces the first appearance of certain symptoms in the child's second year. They are the result of new demands on the child's developing ego, such as the acquisition of sphincter control.

And these demands also produce further conflicts in the oral sphere. For example refusing to eat can be understood as a displacement from the lower parts of the body (defecating and holding back faeces) to the upper parts of the body (eating and refusing to eat).

Fraiberg (1950) regards the sleep disorders in the second year as being the result, among other factors, of the defence against traumatic situations and fear of a danger, both of which are processed in the dream in an anticipatory way. The repetition in dreaming serves to master traumatic situations or to revive pleasurable experiences.

Fraiberg does not make dreams the specific focus of her work, but she describes situations in which sleep disorders occur and sees them as connected with anxiety dreams leading to the child waking up. In her case vignettes the kind of connection between sleep disorders and the dream activity of children becomes clear. The experience of fear in a dream leads to the child waking up and to the sleep disorder just as happens in a traumatic neurosis. The dreamer relives the traumatic scene and the dream-work supports the attempt to anticipate the danger. Reliving the scene matches the tendency to repeat that we can observe in children and that marks both play and dreaming. Fraiberg draws a parallel between repetition in dreaming and the active mastering of a passively experienced danger that the child was threatened by. The transformation from passive into active is the next ego function that is achieved at this age and that helps the child to gain mastery of its fears (Fraiberg, 1950, pp. 308f).

Castration anxiety

The period of life in which sphincter control is *achieved* produces the conflict between the child's pleasure in retaining and pleasure in expelling its faeces, and this conflict may be experienced as castration anxiety. In its turn the fear of *losing* the recently acquired ability to control the sphincter is connected with the fear of object loss, which can also be experienced as castration anxiety. All these are examples for the emergence of new conflicts, of new demands on the psyche, and of the ego developments arising from them. The demands made on the child's psyche by reality and by the instinctual drives are motors for the child's development that can, however, come to a temporary standstill or slide into regression. The development of symptoms is to be understood as a compromise formation between the drive-wish and the fear of object loss.

Similarly Berta Bornstein (1935) describes the sleep phobia of a two-and-a-half year old girl who experienced it as castration anxiety in connection with anal conflicts, anger, and aggression. She describes the symptoms of the little girl: how, for instance, she was afraid of lying down or had fears in everyday contexts, such as the fear of breaking things or of hurting herself, which are easily recognisable as castration anxiety. These were connected with toilet training and the discovery, at almost the same time, of the difference between the sexes. Bornstein comes to the same conclusion as Fraiberg: the conflict between the wish to hold back stools and the wish to soil and to defecate into the bedclothes leads to a fear of being deprived of love, and leads later to the anxiety dreams and the sleep disorders of this little girl who stood upright and stiff as a poker in her cot, holding back her stool. Bornstein invokes, among other sources, the work of Melanie Klein when she writes of the child's desire to steal the contents of the mother's body and incorporate them, a wish that is accompanied by feelings of guilt and later by fears of retaliation (cf. Bornstein, 1935). Here the content of the body (e.g., food) that was incorporated could also represent the father's penis or indeed the child's stool. Bornstein's interpretation is that in the child's imagination the toilet training has robbed her of the penis, of her own faeces, and of the pleasure in her own faeces.

Alongside offering the chance to address questions of theory, concerning ourselves with dreams is of practical interest. Can we make use of children's dreams in clinical practice? Are dreams a completely different instrument from play in child analysis?

Anna Freud repeatedly emphasised that play and dream can be used in child analysis in the same way. Although we cannot make use of free association in our psychoanalytical work with children, typical manifest dreams offer us pointers to their latent content. Anna Freud, too, points out that the presence of a functioning ego in the child is a precondition for our being able to use and interpret its *dreams* (A. Freud, 1957b, p. 98). And she writes that in child analysis we have to rely on aids such as *play* to replace free association (1965a, p. 29).

Case studies

If we turn now to two case studies of pre-school children in which dreams play a part, we shall see that the role of free association can be taken over by the observations of parents who are themselves in analysis. The first case is that of Little Hans described by Freud, and the other is that of Johnny, whose mother is in analysis with Niederland. In both the parents report their children's dreams, and find memory traces and the day's residues that explain the child's dream.

And both case studies, Freud's account of Hans and Niederland's of Johnny, go into the castration anxieties of the two small boys showing that when the children achieve new levels of development the fear of regression can be great.

Johnny

Let me begin with Niederland's report (1957, pp. 190–208), which is the description of the dreams of a boy of just seventeen months. Niederland heard of these dreams from Johnny's mother who was in analysis with him. Dreams are described from the boy's seventeenth to forty-seventh month. Johnny has a brother, Charlie, two years younger and a sister, three years younger. The fact that the mother describes the child's dreams in her own analysis forms a parallel to the Little Hans case.

The first dream at seventeen months is non-verbal. Johnny woke up screaming and it was an hour before he went back to sleep. During the day he had been to the Natural History Museum with his grandmother and had been enthralled by the bears and the buffaloes. The mother assumed that Johnny was having an anxiety dream. Niederland reports a further non-verbal dream when Johnny was twenty months old. His mother was already seven months pregnant with the next child. Johnny woke up screaming, standing up in his cot, and pressing his fist against his teeth. After his mother held him he calmed down and went to sleep again. According to the mother they had been playing an exciting game in which she whirled him around and in the course of the game he had bitten her breast right through her blouse. He had never done this before and his mother, who was surprised and caught off guard by the sudden, unexpected pain, hit him on the mouth and put him down on the ground very abruptly. Johnny saw the pain and the abrupt change in his mother's behaviour; it gave him a shock and he began to cry. His mother thought that during the day while they were playing Johnny had noticed the baby's movements inside her.

As mentioned before, we owe the knowledge of these two waking-up episodes in Johnny's life to his mother's observations. As to the day's experiences that we can regard as equivalents to associations or as the day's residues, we owe these to her report too. This raises the question of how we are to understand his fear without knowing what the content of dream was? We have a pointer in the way Johnny was holding his hand against his teeth. This would seem to show that in his dream he was reliving the situation that was traumatic for him. His initial desire, the aggressive and pleasurable biting, and his mother's unexpected and painful reaction may have been the traumatic elements in his experience. In the first dream what he was probably reliving was the abrupt ending of his pleasure in looking at the large animals in the museum.

From the age of two and half, Johnny began to report his dreams on waking up. The first verbatim report of a dream was when he was lying in bed with acute tonsillitis and a high temperature: "Jimmy was at the waterspray, Jimmy was at the water stream. Estelle was there too" (Niederland, 1957, p. 191).

One can regard this dream as a wish fulfilment dream such as those in Freud's examples of children's dreams. But it seemed to Niederland that the dream was multi-faceted: there was not only a play-fellow called Jimmy but Jim was also the name of Johnny's father: Estelle was not Johnny's but Charlie's nanny. At the time of the dream Charlie, Johnny's younger brother, was eight months old.

But there is also a traumatic element in this dream and that is the water. Two months before he had this dream Johnny had run from the shallow end of the pool right into deep water and gone under. He was pulled out immediately, had burst into tears but it was not a great shock, as Niederland describes it. A few days later he contracted acute tonsillitis. Whether this could have been connected with his experience in the pool we cannot say, but Johnny himself very probably felt a connection. What is interesting is that he had the dream we have described when he contracted tonsillitis for a second time. Niederland sees the dream as connected to birth, nanny, and the sibling situation. The traumatic element is not only to be found in the episode in the pool but equally in the birth of his younger brother and in his jealousy.

There already appear to be certain elements of dream-work in Johnny's dream: all the events (memory traces) that precede the dream, above all the two illnesses, are condensed. We find symbolisation (water as a symbol for birth and the danger that threatens Johnny in the form of his younger brother), wish-fulfilment (while lying in bed with a high temperature and in pain Johnny dreams of a pool and water), and the nanny is there too, perhaps also representing the mother. In the following months, Johnny kept dreaming of water.

When he was four, the oedipal content of his dreams became more marked. The following is the last dream that Niederland described: "one man who is made dead by another man: A little man made the bigger man dead by hitting with a big stone over his head" (Niederland, 1957, p. 207). Johnny recounted this dream and a few others he had had before to his mother and he was very hesitant and ashamed, which was most unusual for him. Before that he had told her what he had dreamt very openly and without any hesitation. The oedipal content in the aggression directed against his father made him hesitate in exactly the way Little Hans had hesitated to report his aggressive impulses towards his father. In this little collection of dreams there is a clear line of development from wish–anxiety dream to elaborated dream content containing nearly all the elements of dream work. The important and life-changing events Johnny has experienced clearly shape his mental and emotional development. These experiences not only appear in his dreams but are processed psychically in dreaming. The central experiences here were the birth of a younger sibling and his own illnesses. One needs to remember that tonsillitis was a serious illness in the fifties with children running high temperatures and feeling really very ill.

We learn of Johnny's dreams from his mother just as Hans' dreams were reported by his father. In the child analyses of pre-school age children dreams are seldom reported by the children themselves. This is not only, as has often been stated before, lacking free association, but also because children have an attitude to past and present that differs from ours. I shall go into this at a later stage.

Little Hans

I wish to offer a brief sketch of the ego development of Little Hans, basing this on the father's reports of the child's dreams (Freud, 1900a). Apart from the early wish dreams Freud describes in *The Interpretation of Dreams*, there are dreams that Little Hans had that are examples for the parallel development of dreams and ego functions.

The development of Hans' phobia can be regarded as a compromise formation of his oedipal conflict. The conflict is externalised and displaced from the father to the phobic object the horse. Veronica Mächtlinger describes this in her introduction to Little Hans (1995, p. 27).

Condensation as a precursor of externalisation forms part of the mechanism(s) of the phobia, but condensation is equally a central element in dream-work as is symbolisation, which is active in the choice of phobic object, the horse. In the minutes kept by Hans' father there are body projections that display Hans' enormous interest in his body and in particular in his genitals. Body projections are also an essential element in dream-work. Hans' interest in the "widdler" is not confined to living beings but also inanimate objects. "When he was at the station once (at three and three-quarters) he saw some water being let out of the engine. 'Oh, look' he said 'the engine's widdling. Where's it got its widdler?' " (Freud, 1909b, p. 9). But by projecting his images of his own body he can differentiate between animate from inanimate objects. "A dog and horse have widdlers: a table and a chair haven't." In this way the widdler becomes an organiser that enables Hans to sort what he sees into things and living creatures, always basing this on the experience of his own body.

Hans' castration complex develops in connection with a direct threat to have his widdler cut off, a threat made by his mother. Freud comments in a footnote added later in 1923 that one must assume "that children construct this danger for themselves out of the slightest hints, which will never be wanting". It is "all the more valuable that in the case of little Hans the threat of castration is reported by his parents themselves, and moreover at a date before there was any question of his phobia" (pp. 8–9). When Hans was three and half his mother threatened him when she caught him with his hand on his penis: "If you do that I shall send for Dr A to cut off your widdler. And then what would you widdle with?" Hans consoled himself, perhaps a little defiantly, with the reply "With my bottom" (Freud, 1909b, pp. 7–8). This is the stage he had reached, not forgetting the birth of his sister, when he was three years and nine months old and his father reported his first dream: "Today when I was asleep I thought I was at Gmünden with Mariedl". (p. 12). Gmunden was where he had spent the summer but the fact that the dream comes six months later clearly expresses his longing for Mariedl. He then adds "not with Mariedl but alone with Mariedl". Mariedl had become the substitute for the mother. He could love her without the oedipal conflicts with his father, and she had also not given birth to a sibling, and so in his fantasy she could belong to him exclusively.

Even in this apparently simple wish dream we can observe not only the wish to recreate the summer in Gmunden, but also the intertwining of complex processes. The dream offers him a way to avoid oedipal rivalry with his father, a substitute for his mother, and a love object for himself; it furthermore takes care of his conflicts by condensing and displacing them, allowing him to sleep undisturbed.

The next dream Freud describes is of the "type auditif", a term he uses for dreams without visual elements. He sees the appearance of speech in dreams as pointing to things heard or said on the previous day. Hans reports "I thought someone said 'Who wants to come with me?' Then someone said, 'Me'. Then he had to make him widdle." (p. 19)

Hans had been playing forfeits for some time now with two girls: the one whose forfeit it is, is sentenced to widdle. The words in the dream could be spoken by his superego and *having to* do a widdle in front of the girls would represent an order which accommodates his exhibitionistic wish. Here too we find a more developed ego than initially supposed. In his dream, Hans uses a reversal into the opposite so that the exhibitionist act of widdling in front of the girls is something he is virtually ordered to do. His exhibitionistic wish becomes a demand from the superego, and he is freed of any sense of guilt. When his father continued to ask about this he said "she says" instead of "someone says" (p. 9). The father assumed that this "she" was one of the little girls with whom Hans played. Hans was still helped to urinate, his trousers were unfastened for him and his penis taken out, and in his dream Hans fantasised about having the girls there. He told his father when he was helping him widdle that the little girls had watched him widdling the year before.

The next dreams that are reported definitely correspond to adult dreams in their use of the full spectrum of dream-work mechanisms. Alongside other manifestations, the Oedipus conflict and castration anxiety are the expression of an age-appropriate ego and superego development. These developments led in Hans' case to the growth of phobic symptoms, but after his fear of castration had been resolved they helped him to tell fantasy and reality apart.

When does dreamwork first appear?

In the opinion of many child therapists, dream distortion appears for the first time around the child's fifth year with the onset of the oedipal conflict. This is also the view of Heinz Hopf (2007), a child therapist who has worked on dreams, when he states that dream-work, that is, condensation, distortion, displacement, reversal into the opposite, and symbolisation, is not possible until the psychical structures are already developed. I for myself contend—and the examples of dreams given here support this in my view—that *every* developmental conflict that emerges from the child's development represents a demand on its psychic life that entails the development of new ego structures.

In 1912 the first woman child analyst, H. Hug-Hellmuth, described the dream of a small boy whose conflict was primarily at the level of his pleasure in exhibitionism. This very early account of a child's dream also shows us another dimension that dreams have for children. Children still have to learn to recognise the unreality of dreams, to tell the difference between what they dreamt and what really happened. The younger a child is, the less developed is its ego and the more difficult it is for the child to grasp and finally accept the unreality of a dream.

Hug-Hellmuth describes the analysis of a dream of a boy of five and half (1912, p. 1ff).

As she writes, she was able "to reveal what was probably the deeper meaning of his dream" because she had "an exact knowledge of his little experiences and of the milieu in which he was growing up, and also because he had stayed at my home for longer periods" (p. 2). The little boy woke up from his dream with the words "A great big bear wants to eat me" (p. 1). The morning after that he told them:

> ... there was a big fence and on the top of it were lots of pointy arrows and the bear wanted to hug me with its front paws. And in the middle of the ceiling there was a great big black blotch, no, a big Patzen (pooh)".

This dream contains a processing of his pronounced pleasure in exhibitionism and his castration anxiety. In the dream analysis Hug-Hellmuth comments on the spikes on the fence, seeing a reference to the bars of the boy's cot and she also recounts an episode in which the little boy had urinated with evident pleasure between two planks in a fence. She sees the *Patzen* on the ceiling as expressing the boy's anal interests. It seems he had smeared his faeces when very young and was still fond of parading his *Patzen* (blots). When he was younger he used to stand up in his cot holding up his nightshirt, which is interpreted as pleasure in exhibitionism. The boy's fear of the bear that wants to hug and eat him (= kiss) is interpreted as the wish to see his father whom he had only seen very sporadically in the preceding months. Hug-Hellmuth also interprets the dream bear as representing the mother: the boy loves to run to meet her and let himself be caught by her.

Although for two years now the child had known that dreams were not real events, he still experienced this dream as reality, and when he woke up he turned to his aunt for protection from the bear. She writes: "He holds on to the reality of the dream because his fear is, basically, a wish that only the dream can fulfill for him" (p. 5). As if the bear had really still been there he wanted to be held by his mother-substitute aunt.

Here too we see how wish-fulfilment and fear are intertwined in the dream and this is the result of dream-work, that is, the result of the boy's ego development. We find here the elements of distortion, reversal into the opposite, and repression although these are not named in these terms by Hug-Hellmuth. Only since Anna Freud's work with her detailed description of ego functions and ego development has it become possible to describe them.

The big bear that envelops and holds the little boy in his dream—which I mentioned above—evokes associations with Lewin's screen dream (Lewin, 1953), described as the all-enveloping maternal breast that makes inside and outside indistinguishable, promises uninterrupted oral satisfaction as the sweet mash in a land flowing with milk and honey, and dispenses with any differentiation of objects. I shall return to this point later.

It is hard for the little boy to recognise the wish-fulfilling function of a dream and its unreality. There was one dream he remembered for a long time, a wish dream, the content of which was a wonderfully decorated Christmas tree that he tried in vain to find when he woke up, and he kept retelling this with the comment: "Well, yes, I was so stupid then, I really believed it was a real Christmas tree: but it was only a dream" (Hug-Hellmuth, 1912, p. 5).

If the dream screen represents the maternal breast then the oral triad, as Lewin terms it, is an essential element of sleep and dreaming. The oral triad consists of eating, being eaten up, and falling asleep (Lewin, 1953). He calls the dream screen a visual memory trail and the breast the first "eating-up organ" that the baby knows. The breast envelops the baby and lulls it into sleep (p. 194). Lewin equates the perception of the maternal belly with the perception of the breast. Leuschner writes on Lewin's concept of the dream screen:

> The screen is not the visual memory of the "maternal breast object" in the literal sense. That would still be thinking in over-concretistic terms. This is not an idea, not a Freudian "Idee", but a reference system emerging from the social experience with the early mother in the infant's organism . . . .. (Leuschner, 2011, p. 131)

Melanie Klein's idea of a ubiquitous children's fantasy of robbing the mother of the contents of her body might also be seen in this framework.

On regression as part of falling asleep, which is a process that takes place in children and adults alike, Leuschner also comments that:

> . . . when people fall asleep they follow the procedure of breast feeding and in this process body fragments enter into a relationship of exchange with maternal part objects and become changed in the sense of a *sujet* transformation. (p. 75)

He attributes these experiences to an "early form of body image" and not to the "phenomenon of mentalisation" (p. 76). Hand and mouth in

Leuschner's view are libidinously cathected in falling asleep, which corresponds to Hoffer's theory of the integration of mouth, hand, and eye.

Hoffer assumes that from the beginning of its second year the small child already has an oral-tactile concept of its own body (Hoffer, 1949, p. 49ff). Leuschner sees the particular libidinous cathexis of mouth and hand on falling asleep as "deriving from a body image retrieved by the regression arising in falling asleep" which " 're-calls' the archaic aspects of the mother–child situation in breast-feeding" (Leuschner 2011, p. 63).

In a note made in 1929, Fenichel also describes fantasies similar to those described by Lewin (Fenichel, 1929, p. 447–450): "the dread of being eaten", namely by the mother, corresponds to oral castration anxieties. These are fears of annihilation that Melanie Klein (1932) understands rather as retaliation anxieties for the child's wish to rob the mother of the contents of her body.

The fear of lying down that some small children feel, and that Fraiberg also describes, was not only the fear of soiling the bed in the lying position and of thus making his mother angry, it could just as well be seen in Lewin's sense (1953) as a fear of oral regression in the anal conflict, and this evokes a fear of dreams in which the mother's breast, which is both wished-for and to be avoided, is present as an oppressive, calming, and orally satisfying memory trace. The dream screen as Lewin describes it occurs in dreams only when the sleeper is in the lying position. The little child described by Bornstein is standing in its cot and unwilling to lie down, screaming in fear and desperately holding in its stool, thus avoiding sleep and with it the wish dream (Bornstein, 1935). One could understand this from what has been previously said as displacement from the lower part of the body to the upper part, and thus the oral triad itself is avoided. The fantasised, unconscious equation of the two body orifices, anus and mouth, are ubiquitous in childhood.

In the Night Kitchen, another book by Maurice Sendak, plays with the themes of sleep and dream (Sendak, 1970). Mickey floats up out of his bed, out of his pyjamas and then sinks down, down, floating naked past his sleeping parents and landing finally in the dough down where the bakers are, and then after many detours lands in a huge bottle of milk. The meaning of the dream screen could hardly find a more apt illustration than the story of Mickey's nightmare, an enormous bottle of milk from out of which Mickey calls "I am the milk and the milk is in me". Everything that happens centres on the enjoyment of milk, then dough, and finally cake.

In a symposium on sleep disorders, Anja Maennchen said:

> The most common sleep disturbance occurs when the ego is obliged to give up the desire to sleep at all because it is unable to inhibit the repressed impulses set free during sleep. This economic factor plays a big part in the sleep phobias of children. (Quoted by Fenichel, 1942, p. 60)

As has already been described, the younger the child is the more we have to have recourse to information from the parents about any traumatic experiences of the previous day, for example, manifest conflicts in toilet training, in order to be able to understand the child's dreams. When a child wakes up out of an anxiety dream and tells his parents, he is completely caught up in the impression made by the dream without being able to grasp the unreality of what happened in it.

What we refer to in the case of older children, adolescents, and adults as the secondary working-over of the dream is very probably not present in the dreams of children under five. This is dependent on the individual state of development of the ego.

The revealing of the infantile memory traces that are so important in the dreams of adults is impossible with children under three years of age. The conflicts that are dealt with in a child's dream are current developmental conflicts, that is, those that are part of the child's developing ego and superego. With adults, the dream content is drawn from both present and past, whereas in small children at the pre-oedipal stage past and present are all in one. The different stages in libidinous development and ego development lie quite close together: they are difficult to tell apart and are always in danger of being hidden and overlaid by regression to earlier stages of development.

What Freud refers to as dream-work in *The Interpretation of Dreams* develops in a child's dreams with the development of the ego. The mechanisms of:

1. condensation
2. displacement or reversal
3. symbolisation

4. distortion
5. and finally the representability of the dream content

are psychic functions in primary process. The representability of dream content refers to its moulding into visual forms that small children find so real that they cannot distinguish them from reality (see above).

The ego-regression in sleep, which is a precondition for sleep of any kind, is responsible for the primary process nature of dreams. The diffuse, immediate discharge of excitation that tolerates no delay in primary process and the motor inhibition that accompanies sleep point to the role of dream as the guardian of sleep. Condensation and displacement as important mechanisms of dream-work arise from the flexibility and mobility of psychic energy, the goal of which is immediate satisfaction. There is no place for rationality or the realistic insights in sleep and dreaming. The connection to reality has to be re-established on waking or, in the case of the little dreamer in Hug-Hellmuth's account, it is not until a few months later that he can realise he had thought his beautiful dream was real. However, it is not only wish dreams that are taken for reality, anxiety dreams too can have such a convincing, overwhelming quality of reality that children can only with great difficulty be calmed down after them or they refuse to go to sleep again for fear of the dream recurring.

Condensation in dreams is a function that we can observe in children's dreams also. But we cannot, as in adult analyses, "undo" the condensation through the use of free association because this means is not at our disposal in child analysis. Residues of the day are also not told to us by the children themselves but in most cases by their parents.

About the wish to sleep: Lewin reports a comment on dreams made to him in a conversation by the Spanish–Argentininan psychoanalyst Angel Garma:

> Angel Garma in a personal communication corroborates the idea that a profusion of manifest content signifies a wish to sleep and states that he has noted a complementary counter-transference effect among Institute students attending his course on dreams. They became so somnolent in classes where much manifest dream material was presented that Garma used pictures instead. The sleepiness did not become evident in classes dealing with other analytic topics. (Lewin, 1948, pp. 227f)

This countertransference phenomenon often hinders us in our analytical work when we are confronted with the dream accounts of patients. The oneroid or dreamlike state of mind that the recounting of dreams often evokes is warded off by children as a regressive phenomenon. Here we meet a hindrance to working on children's dreams in analysis and therapies that is similar to the difficulty encountered over free association.

Writing about children's dreams, Martin Grotjahn says:

Is a child intelligent and willing enough to remember its dreams, the difference between the report of a real dream and a fantasy is only slight. The healthy child with all its longing for pleasure is attached to the very thrilling present and is directed by the pleasure principle towards the future and therefore seldom spontaneously reports about the past. When it awakens the night is gone, is nothing; the need for a new day and new ventures inhibits every tendency to look back. Interest in the past is a very unchildlike attitude and is much more characteristic of the adult. The possibility of obtaining reliable dream material by questioning a child is open to doubt because the suggestibility of young children is enhanced by the leading nature of every question, no matter how carefully it may be phrased, and the material obtained in such a manner is scarcely trustworthy. (Grotjahn, 1938, p. 507)

When I was preparing this chapter on children's dreams I made a number of attempts to ask young children about their dreams, in particular children of pre-school age, and, as no one will be surprised to hear, I had little success. Instead I can only confirm Grotjahn's observations: children are far more drawn to fantasising than to reflecting on dreamlife because of the danger that lurks in dreams of slipping into regression.

Regression has to be avoided; progression, progress is the aim of our treatments, so where development has come to a halt we work to get it in motion again. But we must make the fantasies that children present to us just as welcome as if they were dreams, indeed we can treat and use them in the same way as we would dreams. Information from outside on the residues of the day and on other past events are of particular importance in child analysis and we will naturally make use of any reports and observations coming from the children's parents in lieu of free association. As to interpretations, we will most probably refrain from making any that might frighten a child or that the child would not be able to work-over.

Children in latency have already developed an apparatus of defence, their dreams already display the features of dream-work in ways very similar to adults, and the dreams of adolescents are practically identical in structure to those of adults.

It is not until the end of latency and with the onset of puberty that one can arouse interest in dreams during psychoanalytical treatment. To do this requires a sufficiently stable transference relationship. It is only when regression and hidden, aggressive drive wishes have lost some of their terror that adolescents can give their attention to dreams and use the technique of free association.

Case study

Christine was a fourteen-year-old girl in treatment with me because of extreme, aggressive symptoms. Christine cut herself, repeatedly making deep wounds that had to be treated surgically. After about a year of analytical treatment, coming four times a week, she told me the following dream: she was in an enormous cinema in which the rows of seats were facing the wrong way, with their backs to the screen: a figure rather like one out of a science fiction film made her entrance, a doll-like figure that she herself repeatedly attacked, hitting it really hard. Christine laughed out loud while telling me this and the association she made was that her siblings were like dolls for their mother, that her brother was her mother's baby doll.

Christine suffered from severe sleep disorders: she simply could not go to sleep. I had the impression that she was avoiding sleep in order not to be exposed to the extreme agitation she might feel when her ego, as it were, dissolved at the moment of falling asleep. She also wanted to avoid frightening dreams such as the one just described. Her aggressive feelings caused her enormous feelings of guilt. Again and again there were dream sequences that were terrifying and bloodthirsty and she would cut herself again. The self-harming seemed to be a way out of aggressive tensions that equally left their imprint in the bloodthirsty dreams. Without going further into the content of the dreams I should like to examine their structure: condensation of the whole of the dream happenings, symbolisation (the doll and the cinema), reversal to the opposite (the way the seats were reversed and, not least, her reversed affect while recounting the dream) are elements of dream-work in this dream. Christine's weakened ego could not deal with the tension of her aggression, which was why she chose to mutilate herself as her only way out.

Her dreams, at fourteen, showed all the structural features of adult dreams. But her ego was not strong enough to meet the storm of aggression and drive tension pent up in her.

So far I have concentrated on intra-psychic processes that are hard to distinguish in the early phases of a child's development from real life influences on it. In a way that is similar to these intra-psychic processes, body sensations, pain, or auditive perceptions play a role in the dream story line. They become built into the dream. An example here is the urge to defecate in the case of the little girl who finally tried to avoid sleep, dreaming, and lying down altogether in order not to give way to the urge to defecate and soil herself and her bed.

Leuschner reports a case of a body stimulus dream in a ten-year-old boy who comes to the breakfast table and tells his father that he has just dreamt how there was a truck driving along behind him when its motor suddenly exploded. When his father was interested in hearing more the boy quickly put his hand on his bottom and said he could not say anything now because he urgently had to "do a big one" and rushed off to the toilet (Leuschner, 2011, p. 118). The body sensation in the dream is clear: "the fear of soiling himself or his bed is transformed into a dream of threatening explosion" (p. 119). The combination of a body sensation with lazy delay make up the content of the dream that is, however, transformed "into a highly creative psychic activity in sleep".

Final reflections

Recognising dreams for what they are and not believing they are really happening, like the little boy in Hug-Hellmuth's dream report, is an achievement of the ego, which is of similar importance for the inner life of children as the perception and naming of feelings. It is part of an awareness of inner processes that is just as important as the perception of body processes and functions that finally lead to the development of the body image. Recognising the unreality of dreams helps the child to develop and sharpen his outer and inner perception.

Children's dreams can shed light on their ego-development and this knowledge can guide us on whether and how to use dreams in their treatment. Even though we are seldom given a reliable account of the dreams of children of pre-school age, given the similarity between dream and fantasy in very young children we can draw on their fantasies as a source in treatment in the way we use dreams. A child's dream material can be used to determine what stage it has reached along the developmental lines as conceived by Anna Freud, and, finally, its changing character could be seen as a further developmental line in its own right: the line from wish dream to anxiety dream.

References

Bornstein, B. (1935). Phobia in a two-and-a-half year old child. *Psychoanalytic Quarterly*, 4: 93–119.

Fenichel, O. (1929). Two short supplementary notes. *International Journal of Psychoanalysis*, 10: 447–450.

Fenichel, O. (1942). Symposium on neurotic disturbances of sleep. *International Journal of Psychoanalysis*, 23: 49–68.

Fraiberg, S. (1950). On the sleep disturbances of early childhood. *Psychoanalytic Study of the Child*, 5: 308–309.

Freud, A. (1965a). Normality and pathology in childhood assessments of development. In: *The Writings of Anna Freud, Vol. 6*. New York: International Universities Press.

Freud, A. (1957b). The contribution of direct child observation to psychoanalysis. In: *The Writings of Anna Freud, Vol. 5* (pp. 95–101). New York: International Universities Press, 1969.

Freud, S. (1900a). *The Interpretation of Dreams. S. E.*, 4–5. London: Hogarth.

Freud, S. (1901a). On dreams. *S. E.*, 5: 629–686. London: Hogarth.

Freud, S. (1909b). *Analysis of a Phobia in a Five-year-old Boy. S. E.*, 10: 1–149. London: Hogarth.

Grotjahn, M. (1938). Dream observations in a two-year-four-months-old baby. *Psychoanalytic Quarterly*, 7: 507–513.

Hoffer, W. (1949). Mouth, hand and ego integration. *The Psychoanalytic Study of the Child*, 3: 49–56.

Hopf, H. (2007). *Träume von Kindern und Jugendlichen*. Stuttgart: Kohlhammer.

Hug-Hellmuth, H. (1912). Analysis of a dream of a 5½-year-old boy. *Psychiatric Journal of the University of Ottawa, 11*(1): 1–5.

Klein, M. (1932). *The Psycho-Analysis of Children. The Writings of Melanie Klein, Vol. 2.* London: Hogarth Press, 1975.

Leuschner, W. (2011). *Einschlafen und Traumbildung*. Frankfurt am Main: Brandes & Apsel.

Lewin, B. D. (1948). Inferences from the dream screen. *International Journal of Psychoanalysis, 29*: 224–231.

Lewin, B. D. (1953). Reconsideration of the dream screen. *Psychoanalytic Quarterly, 22*: 174–199.

Mächtlinger, V. (1995). *Introduction to: Freud, S.: Analyse der Phobie eines fünfjährigen Knaben*. Frankfurt am Main: Fischer Taschenbuch.

Niederland, W. G. (1957). The earliest dreams of a young child. *The Psychoanalytic Study of the Child, 12*: 190–208.

Sendak, M. (1963). *Where the Wild Things Are*. New York: Harper & Row.

Sendak, M. (1970). *In the Night Kitchen*. New York: Harper & Row.

CHAPTER TWO

The development of children's dreams

Veronica Mächtlinger

The changes in structure and form, which can be observed in children's dreams in early childhood, especially between the ages of two and five, provide us with important insights into the increasing structural complexity within the child's psychic life. Dream *content* naturally reflects the events of the day, together with the anxieties familiar to us in successive developmental phases, but it is the *structuring* of a dream that throws light upon the evolving and otherwise elusive early mental processes that lead to the building of the child's personality. In my opinion, it is worth examining these structural changes in early dreams as they allow us to make rough estimates of the average age at which these important developments occur, as well as illuminating the manner in which their influence on the child's inner life can be recognised. In doing so, we can observe how the increasing complexity in dream structure reflects a growing psychical complexity as the development of new mental abilities helps the child to structure and organise its inner and outer experience. The interaction between the drives and these evolving inner structures gives rise to the development of ego functions, which increasingly enable the child to deal with conscious and unconscious wishes and to find compromise solutions for fears, affects, and conflicts.

For some people, childhood dreams (often recurring or anxiety dreams) may remain particularly important and are clearly remembered into adulthood, together with a feeling that they have a special significance in their personal development, although their deeper significance usually remains concealed. This becomes particularly clear when childhood dreams play an important part in the analyses of some adult patients. The symbolism in such dreams condenses important themes in the patient's inner life and, in subsequent analytical work, can often be seen to be directly connected with the patient's central, life-long (and unresolved) conflicts and defence mechanisms. Such dreams underline one important function of children's dreams: they serve as a kind of container for deeper conflicts and allow us a privileged insight into a child's direct psychical experience, normally concealed under layers of later psychical development and that, only partially emerges after laborious reconstruction in adult analyses.

I think here of a childhood anxiety dream that held an important place in the analysis of an adult patient, who sought help when her mother fell ill with a life-threatening disease. She described herself as "a very good child" who had, by and large, tried to avoid all conflicts with her mother. A recurring childhood dream had so frightened her that she developed a serious sleeping disorder and was unable to fall asleep.

> A terrifying witch danced every night in the idyllic garden of the country house in which the family had lived. She awoke from this dream very frightened, but was even more afraid of going back to sleep. The witch was a malevolent presence in the garden in which she had always found a refuge—but her greatest fear was that the witch would come into the house. She was only able to contain her fear as long as the witch remained in the garden.

This garden allowed an approximate dating of the dream. The patient must have been between three and a half and five years old when the nightmare led to her sleep problems. Dreams with a similar structure recurred several times during her childhood and adolescence—the witch being replaced by various frightening figures always threatening to break in from the outside and to destroy a peaceful, harmonious situation. At the beginning of her analysis the patient had very little insight into the powerful ambivalence she felt towards her strict, depressive, and now severely ill, mother. Against great resistance she gradually came to recognise her desperate attempts to ward off her own aggression through externalisation and projection, as in the childhood dream.

The fundamental, and still unresolved, conflicts, so graphically depicted in this patient's childhood dream, played a central role in the analytic transference–countertransference process whereby its profound psychic significance in her conflicted inner world and her life became very clear. That such dreams remain so clear has perhaps to do with the fact that the conflicts expressed remained unresolved over years.

Eugene Mahon, in his fascinating clinical paper, "Dreams: a developmental and longitudinal perspective" (1992), also emphasises this important developmental aspect in children's dreams and shows how dreams, over time, reflect the increasing structural and psychic development of the dreamer. He describes three dreams dreamt by a child whom he analysed between the ages of five and ten, and who later, between the ages of thirteen and twenty, returned briefly for consultation. I regret that I cannot go into this fine paper in detail here, but, in summary, Mahon shows how—at the ages of six, thirteen, and twenty—the same infantile wish builds the deepest layer of meaning in the dreams, but also how this infantile element assumes a different form and changing contours according to the developmental phase in which the dream occurs, thereby reflecting and illuminating the ongoing structural changes in the psyche, from the phallic phase to the transformations of puberty and the consolidation in adolescence.

John Mack (1965), focused on anxiety dreams in his enquiry into the development of children's dreams. Anxiety dreams are of especial interest as they reveal what, if any, inner resources are available to a child attempting to cope with great anxiety at different phases of development. Very early nightmares are usually accompanied, on waking, by a complete loss of orientation and the inability to distinguish between inner and outer reality. Dreams of this nature can often be observed towards the end of the first year and during the second year of life. This is a period of development in which—structurally speaking—early ego functions and reality testing are only present, if at all, in very rudimentary form, and self-object differentiation is still precarious. A one-year-old child is therefore helpless in this situation, having few inner resources to help deal with extreme fear and anxiety, and therefore remains dependent on the parents or care-takers to quieten him and help restore his equilibrium. Mack cites anxiety dreams from early childhood into latency and shows how with increasing age the gradually evolving ego develops new ways of protecting itself against anxiety. The greater the anxiety the greater the need to develop defence mechanisms. The developments that can be seen in anxiety dreams therefore tell us more about early defence mechanisms than do wish-fulfilling dreams.

Cecily de Monchaux (1978), in an interesting paper, which I fear is seldom read today, also stresses this organising function of the ego in the child's efforts to gain control over anxiety. Dreams provide not only a container for fantasy content, but in the dream work the ego is actively engaged in trying to convert anxiety and anxiety producing affects into an acceptable form in order to keep them within bounds and under control. When this fails the child awakes from an anxiety dream.

We usually relate our dreams in the past tense: "I had a dream"—in this way we distance ourselves from the immediate dream content, and sometimes we add: "I was so relieved when I awoke to find it was just a dream". Small children are not, at first, able to make these distinctions and it is usually the parents who say, when the child awakes from an anxiety dream: "But it was only a dream". A dreamer may also distance himself by becoming the onlooker or by remaining uninvolved in the dream events. However, in the dream already quoted, such attempts to distance herself from anxiety were clearly not yet available to my patient as a child—the evil intentions of the witch were experienced as being directed at herself. This would seem to indicate that, in these early stages of mental development, even such relatively simple anxiety-reducing mechanisms are not initially available to the child.

As we know, Freud initially thought that children's dreams represented simple wish-fulfilments and therefore regarded them as relatively uninteresting—an opinion that, however, he soon changed. As early as 1911 (in a footnote) he writes, that, "... children soon begin to have more complicated and less transparent dreams", referring thereby to the dreams of Little Hans. In 1916–1917 he makes a still clearer distinction between the dreams of younger and older children and, after again stressing the wish-fulfilling aspect of very early dreams, he writes:

> You must not suppose, however, that all children's dreams are of this kind. Dream-distortion sets in very early in childhood and dreams

dreamt by children of between five and eight have been reported which have all the characteristics of later ones. (p. 125)

He later lowered this age estimate to between four and five years. The distortions in the later dreams, which Freud mentions, are a visible outward sign of those mental developments, with the help of which, the child seeks ways to avoid anxiety and other painful affective states. In contrast to wish-fulfilment dreams, these dreams require interpretation to be understood.

The dreams of Little Hans, referred to by Freud, demonstrate, in outline, these early developments. The first reported dream occurs at the age of three and a half years, and appears easy to understand as the expression of a longing to see the little girl Mariedl and, as Hans stresses, to be "alone" with her. Freud interprets this dream solely with reference to the wish-fulfilling aspect with regard to Mariedl—at least he does not comment further on the dream. However, we know from the father's information that Hans' little sister Hannah had been born just before this dream and that shortly after the birth he had fallen ill and had cried out in his feverish state "But I don't *want* a baby sister!" (Freud, 1909b, p. 11). We might, therefore, surmise that the dream also represented his wish to be alone with his mother (without his sister) and that, through displacement, a compromise solution was sought and found for his disappointment and emerging conflicts.

In the following dreams Freud again does not explore wider ranging possible meanings, but the additional information we have offers increasing evidence for the work of distortion, that is, for the operation of developing defence mechanisms, which are significant in the "later" dreams that come gradually to resemble adult dreams. Disguised wishes become increasingly frequent in Hans' dreams—above all in displacement from the original object to another person, the relationship to whom is apparently less burdened by unconscious conflicts. The wish itself does not yet appear to be conflicted—it is, at first, the object towards whom the wish is directed that has been changed.

At the age of four and a quarter Hans' wishes towards his mother had apparently become more complex and conflicted, and resulted in the following less transparent dream: Hans tells his father, "I say, last night I thought: someone said: 'Who wants to come with me?' Then someone said: 'I do'. Then he had to make him widdle" (Freud, 1909b, p. 19).

When his father asked him to repeat the dream Hans said "she said" instead of "someone said". The dream clearly had to do with Hans' wish that a girl should help him to urinate, something that had afforded him pleasure for some time. Freud connects the significance of this dream with an incident, also reported by the father, occurring in the days before.

> This morning Hans was given his usual daily bath by his mother and afterwards dried and powdered. As his mother was powdering round his penis and taking care not to touch it, Hans said: "Why don't you put your finger there?"
>
> *Mother*: "Because that'd be piggish."
>
> *Hans*: "What's that? Piggish? Why?"
>
> *Mother*: "Because it's not proper."
>
> *Hans* (laughing): "But it's great fun!" (Freud, 1909b, p. 19)

Here, the forbidden and unfulfilled wish that his mother should touch his penis appears in the dream addressed to a girl playmate and, in this form, appears to have found hope of fulfilment. This connection is, however, not immediately obvious from the manifest content of the dream as in the first reported dream.

Shortly afterwards, when Hans was four and three-quarters, he had his first anxiety dream from which we can infer that considerable further inner development had taken place:" When I was asleep I thought you were gone and I had no Mummy to coax with" ("coax" is Hans' expression for "to caress") (Freud, 1909b, p. 23).

Here Freud writes:

> This dream alone points to the presence of a repressive process of ominous intensity. We cannot explain it, as we can so many other anxiety dreams, by supposing that the child had, in his dream, felt anxiety arising from some somatic cause and had made use of the anxiety for the purpose of fulfilling an unconscious wish which would otherwise have been deeply repressed. We must regard it rather as a genuine punishment and repression dream, and, moreover, as a dream which failed in its function, since the child woke from his sleep in a state of anxiety. (Freud, 1909b, p. 118)

Shortly before this dream, the father had described how, for the first time, Hans had not denied the difference between the sexes as he watched Hannah having her bath—although his reaction betrayed a certain bewilderment. "... he began laughing. On being asked why he was laughing, he replied 'Because her widdler's so lovely' " (Freud, 1909b, p. 21).

Freud notes that this dream occurred at the same time as the outbreak of Hans' phobia—his fear of leaving the house, that is, of leaving his mother. The understanding of Hans' phobia is basically the understanding of the anxiety dream. In the course of the analytical work with Hans, the wishes he is struggling against, as they cannot be reconciled consciously with his relationships to his parents, become clearer. The dream and his symptoms are compromise formations seeking a regressive solution for oedipal conflicts and castration anxieties. His fear of his own aggression towards his (beloved) father transmutes into a fear of horses and escalates into the phobia. Hans renounces his drive wishes, internalises the conflict, and withdraws into the inhibitions imposed by his phobia. Expressed in structural–theoretical terms: at the age of four and three-quarters ego and super-ego are already sufficiently established in Little Hans' mental organisation to produce a dream and a neurotic symptom of this kind.

Little Hans' dreams show us clearly the dominant wishes, affects, and conflicts with which he was preoccupied in his developing psychical life. The progression from the transparent wish-fulfilment dreams of very early childhood to the later distorted dreams reflects the extensive mental development at this period of his life.

As we all know, considerable differences of opinion exist among the various psychoanalytical theories on the question of the age at which such inner mental processes emerge and develop. At what stage can an infant have recourse to organised mental systems capable of defending effectively against anxiety? Are such capabilities present very early—as some theories suggest—or should we rather think in terms of gradually unfolding processes, in which several factors such as the child's constitution, early experience, and the nature of the environment in which it develops, contribute to shaping and moulding a relatively stable organisation of mental structures which develop as maturation proceeds? I use the word "structure" here to designate a stable, gradually developing mental system in which successive differentiations also reflect maturational and developmental changes in perceptual and cognitive abilities, which, in interaction, result in the increasing complexity of intra-psychical reality. The earliest affective interaction between mother and baby provides the context for these developments during which self and object representations take shape and result, by way of internalisation processes, in a relatively stable structural organisation, which encompasses the individual's complex developmental history.

For this reason, it seems worth looking more closely at the changes in dream activity in very small children, in whom these mental structures are still in the process of development and would therefore be reflected in the ways in which the dreams are constructed. While preparing this talk I came across the following sentence in Freud's *The Interpretation of Dreams*: "These considerations may lead us to feel that *the interpretation of dreams may enable us to draw conclusions as to the structure of our mental apparatus* . . . I do not propose, however, to follow this line of thought" (Freud, 1900a, p. 145, my italics).

I would like to follow this thought by examining an unusual continuous sequence of early dreams described by Niederland (1957). As mental structures evolve, the increasing complexity of the dreams becomes apparent. An examination of these changes can therefore be an invaluable aid in our search for the "beginning of observable mental activity", as Freud described it (Freud, 1916–1917, p. 126).

Perhaps, in following this lead, the boundaries of clinical speculation might become clearer, which, in turn, could perhaps safeguard us against attributing to the infant complex psychical functions that cannot, at least in any organised form, be present at this very early stage of development. We sometimes, perhaps, have a tendency to extrapolate too hastily from later developmental phases to very early inner processes.

Niederland's article allows us to share the first dreams of a little boy, Johnny, whose mother had earlier been a patient of his in analysis, and whom he describes as an intelligent and reliable observer. Johnny, a cheerful, bright child seemed to be developing "normally" in a stable, intact family. His mother was able to record the dreams on the day they were dreamt, filling in details of what was going on in the child's life, his experiences, and the affects connected with them (cf. Freud, 1900a, and Anna Freud, 1936). This additional information contributed, as is usual in very early dreams, to their understanding. The dreams were neither directly nor indirectly interpreted. The growth in complexity of Johnny's dreams is vividly described and, as in Hans' dreams, they are clearly associated with everyday situations of conflict and traumatic events. The dreams illustrate clearly the manner in which the developing ego, when under pressure, attempts to deal with anxiety and conflicts. Altogether eleven dreams covering a period of thirty months are described, from the time Johnny was one and a half to nearly four years old, thus providing us with a rare long-term sequence of early dreams and making it possible to examine successive developments in the form and structure of the dreams over time.

Four-year-old Johnny was the eldest of three children. His two brothers were born during the period of the dreams described, Charlie after Johnny's second birthday and Sandy three months after he turned three. Obviously many of his dreams centred around the mother's two pregnancies and on the difficulties Johnny had in coping with the arrival of his two siblings. Towards the end of the series we see the beginnings of an oedipal conflict. Johnny's dreams deal unremittingly with the inner and outer conflicts that preoccupy him but also increasingly address the deeper, conscious and unconscious conflicts characteristic of the age and stages of development.

The first two dreams were non-verbal nightmares. From the first dream, at seventeen months, he awoke screaming, and it took some time for his parents to calm him down. On the day before he had paid his first visit to the Natural History Museum and was fascinated and excited by the large animals—the bears, buffaloes etc., and could hardly be persuaded to leave the museum.

From the second dream—at the age of twenty months—he again woke up screaming. His mother found him standing up in his cot pressing his right fist against his teeth. Once more she was able to soothe him and he went back to sleep. The mother was then seven months pregnant and on the previous evening she had played wild games with Johnny, which he had thoroughly enjoyed. Suddenly while playing he bit her nipple and hurt her, which he had never done before—she put him down and, also for the first time ever, slapped him. Johnny burst into tears. His mother thought that he might have bitten her because he had felt the movements of the baby. The gesture of pressing his fist against his teeth brought this incident to her mind.

At two and a half, Johnny reported his first verbal dream. Johnny woke and loudly and with pleasure announced: "Jimmy was at the waterspray (fountain). Jimmy was at the waterstream. Estelle was also there." Jimmy was a friend he enjoyed playing with at a fountain in the playground. He had, however, been ill for three days with acute tonsillitis and had not been allowed to go to the playground as he had wished. The dream was then—as was the case with Hans' early dreams—a wish-fulfilment after a frustration. But this was obviously not the whole story. The friend had the same name as Johnny's father and the woman in the dream was a children's nurse who had helped his mother following Charlie's birth. He had seen her in the park breast-feeding her own child. The themes—birth, breast-feeding, and siblings—are all hinted at in the dream. A traumatic incident two months before this dream may also have been relevant. He had jumped into the deep end of a swimming pool and gone under, but his father had pulled him out immediately. He was shocked and had cried but otherwise the incident did not seem to have any further effect. A few days later he developed acute tonsillitis and ran a high temperature.

Subsequently, at the zoo, he developed a keen interest in the sea-lions, admiring their swimming skills, and was interested in how they could stay under water for so long. At home in his bath he imitated their sounds and exclaimed "I'm a sea-lion!" These were clearly attempts to actively work through and deal with the swimming pool trauma. Otherwise his love of water remained unchanged, but during the following summer at the seaside he was anxious and talked about the time "when my head was under water" and called the water in which this had happened "bad water".

Water figured in many of Johnny's dreams. He had always enjoyed playing with water but in his dreams water increasingly refers to the theme of birth. The fourth dream, at two years ten months, he related to his mother as he woke up: "I saw a child in a tunnel—the child fell into the water". In contrast to his usual open and clear speech his voice was low and he mumbled. His mother was again pregnant, which he had noticed, and on the day before the dream he had talked a lot about the new baby. When asked about the child in the dream he first said that he did not know who it was and then, that it was his brother Charlie, and finally that it was himself. After a pause he added: "I fell into the water; Daddy took me out". The dream seems to contain a reproach to the mother—referring not only to the past but also to the future—and appears to express the child's resentment over this fresh pregnancy and the new baby.

In the last two weeks of the pregnancy Johnny reported three water dreams:

I had a special kind of sleep. It was raining and there was water jumping up and down, up and down. There were cars coming in the street, jumping up and down. There were cars coming in the street, many cars.

All three dreams had these repeated elements, lots of rain, many cars. His experience of the rain in his dreams was so powerful that he insisted on getting up to see the rain from the window (it was not in fact raining). Later, the meaning of the many cars became clearer when he told his father about a gang of children who had invaded the playground and disturbed him and his friend at play. The many cars appeared to be a symbol for the many unwanted children (siblings) who deprived him of everything, his mother, food, toys, and playground. The day before one of these dreams, he had sat on his mother's lap for a while. She thought that he had again felt the baby moving inside her as he suddenly said: "The baby is inside you, around you, all around".

Johnny was very interested in the preparations for the new baby and went in to the baby's room several times to check whether it had not secretly arrived. Sometimes he announced that he himself was a baby, crawled around, and spoke baby talk. His mother then went to hospital and returned a week later with his brother Sandy. Two weeks after her return—Johnny was now three and a quarter years old—he spent the night at his grandmother's. On that day he had taken over Charlie's buggy, refusing to give it up, saying: "I'm a little baby, I am Charlie, I'm Charlie ...". He only agreed to relinquish it when his grandmother promised she would travel with him to her house by subway—which he loved doing. He slept in his grandmother's room. He woke up suddenly in the night and cried out, "A parakeet bit me in my hand", and pointed to his hand. He begged to be allowed to sleep in his grandmother's bed and went back to sleep. But when he woke the next day and saw his grandmother lying asleep in the bed he had occupied, he exclaimed, "Get out of the bed, grandma! There is a parakeet in the bed. He will bite you!", and later added:

The parakeet flew out of the tunnel zoo from the cage where the sealions are. The parakeet flew first to my house. He did not find me in my house, because I slept in grandma's house. The parakeet then flew all the way to grandma's house into my bed and bit me in the hand. He came in through the window.

In the zoo, near the sea-lions, was an aviary with exotic birds, including parrots. A few days before there had been some disturbance, and the birds had flapped their wings violently against the bars of the cage and screeched. In addition, on walks after Charlie's birth, Johnny had always wanted to go down one particular road because he was fascinated by a parakeet in a cage in a window. Sometimes the cage held several parakeets and this fact interested him greatly. "Where did the other parakeets come from? Were they new parakeets?"

We can understand this dream as an expression of Johnny's wish to be rid of too many new siblings and his resulting fear of punishment, which pursues him relentlessly although he is not in his own bed.

Here—as with Little Hans—we observe an internalisation of the conflict and an indication of an early precursor of superego development. Whether Johnny experiences guilt feelings at this point, or whether his hostile feelings towards his siblings have led to a fear of losing his mother's love we cannot say, but the parakeet does to him what he had done to his mother.

In the last dreams reported, however, a further development has taken place and guilt feelings become clearer. These dreams are concerned with the questions of where children come from, with castration anxieties, the fear of death, and finally with oedipal themes that emerge in an unmistakable form.

At three years and eleven months old Johnny dreamt: "Rose had a new puppy. The puppy was white. It was talking and jumping up and down on the bed. Then the puppy was running and broke a leg." A little later he changed this to: "The puppy's leg broke off. It was dead and could not walk and could not talk."

This dream condenses many internal and external events, and we cannot but be impressed by the extensive dreamwork involved. Rose was the mother of a friend. The jumping dog is a symbol for Charlie who jumped up and down in his bed and disturbed Johnny, as he had already complained to his parents. Moreover, a few days previously he had tested his mother by declaring that he very much wanted to have a new sibling. His mother, who understood him, assured him that even if *he* wanted another sibling *she* did not, because then she would not have enough time to take care of him and his brothers properly. Johnny was delighted with this reply and repeatedly reported it to others adding the reason his mother had given. In addition an uncle of his had broken his leg skiing and Johnny had been much preoccupied with the plaster cast and talked about it a great deal. His friend, an only child, had a dog that followed him everywhere just as Charlie followed Johnny, which was also something he had complained about and he had commented on a limping dog in the street. The family had that day been talking about Washington's birthday and Johnny was very puzzled and made somewhat anxious by the fact that it was Washington's birthday and yet, at the same time, he was dead. (Preparations were also being made for Johnny's fourth birthday). On a visit to the museum in the days before he had for the first time realised that the large stuffed animals that so fascinated him were dead. This worried him and he said: "When I die, I don't want to be dead".

In this extremely condensed and complex dream it seems that Johnny's increasingly hostile wishes towards Charlie and his wish that he should lose a leg and die had intensified his own fear of dying. The dream detail that Rose had a "new puppy" contains a hint that the hostile wishes had come to include, and were also directed towards, his youngest brother, Sandy.

The next dream—a week later—shows unconcealed oedipal content. Johnny wanted at first to relate the dream to his father but then hesitated and said he would tell him later. It took some time before he said: "Tonight I was a pigeon and I was flying". Later he added, "I was not really a pigeon. It was just a dream".

Two days later Johnny reported the last dream of the series. Once again he was reluctant to do so and kept saying "I don't want to tell you", but eventually he said: "I had another daddy", and later he added "the daddy was taller than you". Johnny had often expressed the wish to be taller and stronger than his father and in the dream he had apparently fulfilled this wish and taken his father's place.

These frankly oedipal themes also cast light on the themes of injury, castration, and death that had so preoccupied him in the preceding dreams. In addition to sibling rivalry, hostility, and the preoccupation with birth themes we recognise the typical symbols and characteristics of the oedipal situation: the wish to fly as a direct expression of an oedipal wish as well as the well-known symbols for castration anxiety. Acute conflict with regard to these oedipal wishes has apparently not yet developed, except perhaps in the growing fear of dying, and the castration theme is largely expressed in relation to others.

A little while later the mother sent Niederland a further dream: "One man who is made dead by another man. A little man made the bigger man dead by hitting him with a big stone over his head." On the day after the dream Johnny talked about David and Goliath and hummed a song from Porgy and Bess he had just learnt: "Little David was small but oh my, he slew big Goliath who lay down and dieth...".

This unusual and fascinating chronological sequence of dreams, stretching over a period of thirty months of the early development of a *normal* child, focuses our attention on the early stages of a child's mental and psychosexual development. Unavoidably, the picture is somewhat fragmentary as we cannot of course assume that Johnny had no other dreams that he did not relate.

With the help of the reported dreams and the associated information about the happenings in Johnny's life, we have been able to follow the structural changes in the dreams in the course of their development:

1. From the early, non-verbal anxiety dreams, which interrupted sleep and are difficult to understand but which were expressed in acute anxiety states that flooded a psyche that had no adequate inner means of protecting itself, and in which no organised and functioning mental structures are discernible.
2. Through the increasingly complex and non-transparent dreams, concerned with coming to terms with traumatic events, with the pressure of repeated pregnancies and the birth of siblings, as well as with increasing conflicts associated with sibling rivalry.
3. Up to the rivalries and preoccupations of the phallic stage and the beginnings of oedipal themes.

This dream sequence from the life of a child developing normally in a stable family has given us pointers to mental developments that, in time, helped the child to cope with the increasingly complex inner and outer world in which he is maturing and growing. In the course of these developments we have been able to mark important stages.

> At two and a half years his cognitive and language development enabled him to express his dream verbally and in symbolic form.

> Towards the end of the second year manifold distortions in the manifest content of the dreams pointed to the early development of ego

defence activity, illustrated in the conflicts associated with hostile feelings towards his mother and younger siblings.

At first no internalisation of the growing conflicts is perceptible. Initially his wishes confront Johnny with difficulties because of his fear of losing his mother's love. In time this fear of loss of love seems, together with a retaliatory fear of punishment, to contribute to an internalisation of the conflict. Punishment dreams indicate precursors of superego formation as shown in the dream of being pursued by the parakeet.

Towards the end of the series, around Johnny's fourth birthday, his dreams are preoccupied with his increasingly powerful phallic and oedipal wishes to vanquish his father and take his place, setting the stage for the development of familiar oedipal conflicts and castration anxieties.

The examination of dream development in the dreams of both Johnny and Little Hans shows us that between the second and fourth year of life the mental structuring processes, which are crucial to the building of the child's personality structure, seem to have developed in an early organised form. In both children early development appeared to be normal, without any major disorders or traumatisation. The developments described do not therefore appear to have been distorted by extraneous interference.

We rarely have such privileged access to comparable detailed dream material, together with information about the associated daily events in the life of a child—information, in the absence of free association, crucial to understanding the dreams of a young child—and can be grateful for this opportunity of examining the gradual development of the mental abilities and processes that are involved in the increasingly complex making of dreams.

References

Freud, A. (1936). *The Ego and Mechanisms of Defence*. London: Hogarth Press, 1937.
Freud, S. (1900a). *The Interpretation of Dreams*. S. E., 4–5. London: Hogarth.
Freud, S. (1909b). *Analysis of a Phobia in a Five-year-old Boy*. S. E., 10: 1–149. London: Hogarth.

Freud, S. (1916–1917). *Introductory Lectures on Psycho-analysis. S. E., 16.* London: Hogarth.
Mack, J. E. (1965). Nightmares, conflict and ego development in childhood. *International Journal of Psychoanalytic Psychotherapy, 46*: 403–428.
Mahon, E. J. (1992). Dreams. A developmental and longitudinal perspective. *Psychoanalytic Study of the Child, 47*: 49–65.
Monchaux, C. de (1978). Dreaming and the organizing function of the ego. *International Journal of Psychoanalytic Psychotherapy, 59*: 443–453.
Niederland, W. (1957). The earliest dreams of a young child. *Psychoanalytic Study of the Child, 12*: 190–208.

CHAPTER THREE

A child is playing, a child is dreaming*

Florence Guignard

Introduction

Freud considered *dreaming* as the guardian of sleep (Freud, 1900a). Such a condensed formulation pinpoints the economic role of *dream activity*: as an intermediate space between drives and reality, *dreaming* is the key means to reach a hallucinatory realisation of unconscious desires. Hence, such a space for *dreaming* plays a prominent role in helping an adult—fairly normal/neurotic—to bear the frustrations endured in external reality.

Is it so for the young child? Does *dream activity* play an economic function as well?

To propose a tentative answer to such a question, we have to specify which age range we are going to study, and, last but not least, to define "what it is that we name a dreaming activity".

I shall consider here the *dream activity* of the child from two to six years old, that is, as soon as verbal activity becomes fairly structured, and before the so-called decline of the Oedipus complex brings in its wake a new necessity to combine splitting and repression to reinforce the reality principle. It is a period of life when secondary processes

---

*Translation revised by Ariane Bégoin.

and defences are not yet fully structured. Thus, mental life seizes every opportunity to utilise all the space needed in order to grow and express itself.

In contrast to this well-known observation, the usual opinion is that children of this age only report raw images of dreams, without action or development in space and time.

Such a restricted point of view might be taken into consideration for children from two to four. However, we should extend our investigation to the narrative of much more than the dream of the night. Not only because language has not yet reached its full development within the age range considered here but, more widely, because the psychoanalyst's listening has to deal with the entire scope of the narrative of compromises between fantasy life and external reality.

Should we follow Freud and Bion to consider such a larger scope of investigation, how do we reach the point in listening to young children?

Playing as dreaming

Shortly after Freud, Melanie Klein defined *playing* as an equivalent to *dreaming*, as far as young children are concerned (Klein, 1923). From then on, child analysts, Anna Freud (1927) and Winnicott (1971) to begin with, largely share this opinion. Later on, many authors added to it when studying *drawing* among young children (e.g., Anzieu, 2004).

Indeed, when looking at, and listening to, a young child, it quickly becomes obvious that every spontaneous activity has a "dreaming" quality that proposes to the observer an incomparable blend of primary and secondary ways of psychic functioning, in logics as well as in the ways of defences.

Example one

For the first time, a little boy, just two-and-a-half years old, was about to spend three nights in a row at his grandmother's. Every morning during the week before this, he played at getting his little suitcase packed, ready to go to his grandmother's. On arriving, he ran happily into the bedroom that was to be his—he was quite familiar with it, because he had stayed there before, but for shorter periods. Suddenly, he said in a half-worried, half-questioning tone of voice, "There's a wolf in the table . . ." His grandmother came closer and asked him, "What does the wolf look like?" "Oh, it's a 'nice-not-wicked' wolf!" was the boy's reply. His grandmother looked at the veining of the marble table that the little boy was pointing to, and said, "Yes, you're quite right. It is there, well contained in the table. Later on, we'll see if we'll talk to it a bit . . ." The little boy, happy and relaxed, went off to play with some toys. That evening, grandmother and grandson said goodnight to the "nice-not-wicked" wolf; thereafter, everybody had a good night's sleep—hopefully, the wolf as well. The veining of the marble table had contained the anxiety about the grandmother's unknown third-party, and the negation "nice-not-wicked" was a good compromise to avoid a more intense form of negation or even denial, such as the grandmother being tempted to justify her good qualities by saying, "No, I don't have any wolves here!" Such a denigration would have forced the little boy to keep his fear of the unknown to himself. Here, the interpretation of the situation took place at a normal iconic level, through a "quasi-play"; language in this case was a kind of "malleable medium" (Roussillon, 1995) with no attempt at making any statement about psychic content as such.

From dreaming to reverie

This example shows a kind of "epidemic" way of functioning: grandmother goes on using the same "dreamy" way of talking as the child does. What does such an observation teach the psychoanalyst? W. R. Bion was the one who understood how large the span of Freud's work on dreams was. By observing the relationship of mothers with their newborns and very young children, he extended the Freudian concept of "dreaming" to a proper capacity of these mothers, and then, to that of the analyst.

To name it, he mixed both English and French languages, and this gave the now well known "capacity of reverie" (Bion, 1962), although it might well be that such a concept is victim of its popularity, and that its content is not so well understood. First, its origins are not always understood as being a compromise between the "adult" and the "infantile" (Guignard, 1996) way of thinking of the mother, who thus tries to find the right level of communication with the way of psychic functioning of her very young child. The *dreaming* mother—*vs.* analyst—

accepts to be a psychic container for the child's sensuous, sensorial, and emotional experiences; by letting them "soak" her mental functioning, a more acceptable means of thinking them will sooner or later be borne in the field of the relationship and passed on to the child.

Bion stresses the fact that dreaming is not only the guardian of sleep, but also the guardian of the whole psychic life (Bion, 1970), as it is the melting pot where "sensuous" and "sensorial elements" can be transformed into "elements to think". Thus, the mother's "capacity of reverie" is discovered to be the prototype of the "capacity of thinking".

Together with her bodily remembrance of the foetus that occupied her body for nine months, the mother's capacity of reverie will give birth to her own capacity to "feel". She will get images from her infant, and help the latter to increase its capacity to "feel quite like her", that is, in *projective identification*. As long as such an experience develops properly, it enhances her own capacity to exert her *attention* to contain/understand what is going on and, through projective identification, the infant's capacity of attention increases as well. A kind of "emotionally experienced image" takes place among each of them, with differences and similarities of course, and such an image shall play its manifold role in the memory of both protagonists.

Attention within the first encounter

Attention can be considered as a "qualification of the life and death instincts" through the introjection/projection process (Freud, 1918b, 1923b). To deny its presence in the newborn child could lead to many damageable misunderstandings, and to a danger of later inhibition in the expression of his psychic life. However difficult it might be to imagine exactly the phylogenetic origins of such a function, the fact is that a human being will only develop his superior psychic competencies if he is given the minimum response to his spontaneous attention by an adult psyche during a sufficient time after his birth. This is particularly true for his creativity and his "fabric of feelings".[1]

Indeed, the newborn has to find enough attraction in this as yet unknown world in order to respond to it with the full strength of his drives. Attention is the expression of the drive's strength. It is the qualitative aspect of appetence, and the first expression of desire that brings the newborn to "take inside something from outside", along with the biological pattern of sucking.

The first *attentive meeting* requires that parents should find more pleasure than fear within the ineffable quality of such a meeting with the unknown of their newborn. Denying the newborn's capacities of attention has something to do with the fear of the uncanny (Freud, 1919h).

Winnicott's concept of "the mother's normal illness" (1958) is implying this preconscious meaning of an uncanny shared by the mother and the newborn.

However, such a meaning often remains out of reach for the other person in the newborn's environment, namely the father. He will keep on denying the attention competencies of this dangerously challenging *in-fans*,[2] a menace for his *homo sapiens sapiens* identity, that gives verbal communication an utmost value.

Needless to say, the above description is rather important, considering the encounter between an analyst and a patient, whatever age the patient is.

Dreaming when talking to the child

Edouard Claparède, a pioneer in the field of psychology and education, used to say "Playing is the child's work." Such a pertinent remark implies that the child has a capacity of *attention* comparable to that of a workman. The child's work consists in discovering both himself and the world around him, through a constant to-and-fro weaving between spaces that are not yet clearly external or internal to himself. Object relations will grow through sense impressions that will need *dreaming and playing* to become *thinking and acting*.

In each true encounter, whether with an adult or a child, the analyst will meet the whole set of primary and secondary defences of the patient with her own. However, those primary ways of functioning—splitting, denial, idealisation, projective identification—will never be discarded or disavowed, only, at best, presented with an alternative vertex, to help the child simultaneously construe an external and an internal reality, as shown in the above example.

Example two

A child is about to go to bed.

Child: Please, Mummy, leave the light on, I am frightened in the dark!

Mother: Why?

C: There are "wicked ones . . ."

M: No, no! There aren't any wicked ones here!

C: Yes, there are!

M: Well, you know, Daddy and I, we shall protect you . . .

We have here a lovely example of a *dreaming* interaction between a young child and his mother: from a secondary logical point of view, there is no need to protect the child if "wicked ones" do not exist. But if the mother is in close contact with her own infantile (Guignard, 1996), she *knows* that there are always "wicked ones" somewhere, even if these are not in the outside world. And the child *feels* that these "wicked ones" have something to do with his being alone in his room while the parents are together—the "grown-ups" should not need to be together, they are strong people, not like him!

Because, when she was a child, she also happened to be frightened, the mother in this vignette functions under a double belief: the conscious one (there are no "wicked ones" here) and the unconscious one (the "wicked ones" *do* exist). She tries to reassure her child—and maybe also her own Infantile—through *negation*: no, no, Daddy and Mummy will not be the "wicked ones" who will look after each other instead of their darling little child in fighting the "wicked ones . . ."

The parents know that they are able to do several things at a time, look after their children as well as have a loving relationship together, work, enjoy their environment, society, and culture. The life of "grown-up" people is interwoven with a multiplicity of simultaneous interests and activities, but do they still remember their childhood frights?

The psychoanalyst knows that the child is frightened by what the intimacy of his parents awakes in him. A little girl I know pretty well used to say, "Oedipus hit again!"

In my second example, the mother's speech evolves throughout her dialogue with her child. She first denies the existence of "the wicked ones" the child is afraid of, then she ends up promising to protect him against them, thus acknowledging their existence. The whole narration has to be considered within the scope of a reverie and not of a Cartesian discourse.

Playing and reality

If the reverie could be considered as a spontaneous tendency of the "good enough" mother (Winnicott, 1956), playing could well be the favourite *malleable medium* of the father (Roussillon, 1995). Together, they form two main vertices for the development of the child's psychic life.

However, sex and death are part of human destiny, and the ghosts of rape and death quickly come to the fore. The psychoanalyst knows that death anxiety is part of the psychic way of functioning. No need to exceptional catastrophes in order to feel such anxiety; it is sufficient to be born and have experienced a normal rhythm of separations and retrievals in order to be ready for the internal discovery of otherness of one's first love objects and, consequently, of the elements of one's Oedipus complex.

Example three

A news item—"A child was kidnapped while the parents were sleeping. Police are actively searching for the kidnapper."

Parents are caught up by reality. How can they reassure their child without denying reality? Later on, when the child will walk to school by himself, how will they keep on reassuring him about "the wicked ones" while at the same time warning him against the dangers of external reality?

The child was right to be worried: the "wicked ones" *do* exist! For instance, the kidnappers.

Here again, the reverie of the parents will help them bring the child to believe them when *they* speak of the "wicked ones" of the external reality.

What I aim at here is to stress the importance of *the thinking process of reverie* in the adult to help the child make the difference between fantasy and external reality. Incidentally, the endemic diffusion of "virtual reality" does not help the parents' generation supposed to educate and protect young children in our present civilisation.

Example four

Playing and dreaming: a session of analysis with a young child.

Paul, nearly three years old, rushes into the consulting room, gets hold of the doll's dinner set and the modelling clay, and invites his (female) analyst to a private dinner; he refuses with great energy the idea of other "toy-people" coming and sharing this "meal". He pours water into two cups, generously watering the whole table in the same movement, makes sausages and pancakes with the clay, gives his therapist some to "eat", and "eats" some himself. He then vigorously plants a small stick into one of the pancakes. But the stick breaks inadvertently. Paul stops at once, examines the break, and looks at the therapist with a puzzled face. She looks back at him with a silent, attentive face. Paul chooses the biggest part of the broken stick and goes on pushing it into the clay; he does so with as much determination as before, but with more concentration and care. He now observes, like an artist, the hollows made in the clay and, with supreme delicacy, takes a small pebble that happens to be lying around, and puts it into one of the hollows. As the analyst is still held by the delight of what she understands, logically enough, as the expression of Paul's desire to make a baby with her, the little boy gets hold of the clay pancake, throws it on the floor, stamps on it, then sits on it and squashes it thoroughly with his bottom, wriggling and uttering suggestive noises of defecation. Then, with a languishing demeanour, he goes to the toy box, chooses a little rag-doll, and lies down on the couch with the doll on his heart, sucking his thumb.

This scene occurs in the first session after a weekend. Paul has had about three months of therapy, three times a week. It has probably been understood that Paul is not a psychotic child.

If we include the Kleinian point of view on early oedipal configurations in our tools for understanding the material, Paul's dreaming/playing activity appears to develop here along a rather classical span of Oedipal desires and defences. To have sex, to fertilise, and to give birth, both with the mother and the father, co-exists with sadistic oral, anal, urethral, and phallic drives that are openly expressed. He shows expressions of love both for the maternal mother and for the feminine mother, as well identification to the fertilising father.

As it is the case in adult patients, we can observe regressive movements throughout the session. We can also appreciate the economic function of Paul's primal fantasies in the *hic et nunc* of that session, after a weekend separation. In what appears both as an actualisation and a denial in the transference of the different aspects of human destiny, Paul "jumps" from one place to another on the stage of the human condition.

The "private dinner" is particularly expressive of the problems of loss of the primary object and of efforts to control it through anal and phallic control, jointly with the straightforward expression of a sexual genital desire for his analyst, with the castration problem associated to it. The anal and urethral components of his oedipal configuration appear, both in his making suggestive sausages, and in his generously spreading water; his desire for phallic domination is expressed through his introducing the stick into the play; his castration anxieties are present when he breaks that stick. All the levels of infantile sexuality are thus expressed in this picture of "little Oedipus before the classical Freudian Oedipus".

However, there is still much to think about Paul's movements in this session.

To give an idea of the "dreamy" associativity of the young child, we could try to put in words what Paul tried to work through in the episode of the broken stick. It would be something like this:

> I had tried to eliminate all the "bad ones". Still, there is undoubtedly one who succeeded in hiding, and he broke my stick just when I wanted to show her how strong I am! Well, I can still make holes with this tiny stick . . . and I can put seeds in the holes.

Just at that point, we can observe a disruption in Paul's associativity: some sensorial element—maybe already represented preconsciously?—is strongly repelled by Paul's consciousness; such a rejection gives way to a quite spectacular regressive disorganisation: the "baby/seed" supposed to be a "gift" for the analyst has become a "shit/baby".

After this disruption, we observe a sudden acceleration of rhythm and action, as well as a complete reversal of the emotional situation. The "baby" given to the analyst seems to be *associated* to the "rival baby of the weekend" and brings to the fore the father image who took his analyst away from Paul during the weekend. Here, Paul is confronted to a failure of his fantasy of seduction, hence to his castration and his infantile helplessness: no, he is not the one who is able to make a child with his analyst; she looked for somebody else to get one. Paul is only a "shit-baby" who has been defecated by an indifferent mother, and this is what Paul is now putting on the stage.

We observe a twofold movement at that moment of the session: on the one hand, Paul regresses to an anal expression of his genital desire;

on the other hand, he identifies himself with the lost object by acting, on the stage of the session, this extraordinary defecation/birth of a baby. However, a new scenery is in preparation: Paul then identifies with a mother taking good care of her baby, and shows one more degree of regression, introducing oral satisfaction to erase (deny?) the primal scene from which he was excluded. At the end of the session, Paul is lying on the couch, sucking his thumb, and cuddling the rag-doll. Autoerotism is trying to heal the phallic–narcissistic wound with a movement of identification to the femininity and the maternal qualities of the mother.

From the point of view of interpretation, the relatively easy understanding of such a material does not give us the slightest guarantee for the know-how of its interpretation. Certainly, this interpretation will be worth being spoken of only if it is given in the transference, but nothing is more difficult than to express feelings and desires—see art and literature. The analyst's capacity of reverie will have to be particularly accurate in order to put into words the desires and feelings that are revealed to him, the analyst being a representative of early childhood parents, and the patient being unaware of this displacement.

Who could decide whether playing or daydreaming was the leader of the dance in this ordinary analytic session with a young child?

However, the general atmosphere of the session is characteristic: non-verbal communication is paramount, which requires from the analyst a certain degree of complicity, the capacity to accept not to know, not to understand immediately, and, above all, not to enclose in a "basic assumption group" (Bion, 1948) verbal formulation any progressive or regressive movement in the session.

Dreaming and drawing

The child begins to draw around the age of three, while his activity of playing is already well established. From three to six or seven, the analyst will enjoy trying to understand as many playing as drawing material. Hence, let us now give some description of the dreaming quality of communication within the activity of drawing.

Example five

A four-year-old boy is drawing with several bright colours. He suddenly sees a black felt-pen, takes the cap away, and draws some small lines, while saying: "One shall not skip this nice colour!" The observer makes an interrogative face. Immediately, the child lengthens the lines all around the sheet, commenting: "This makes a nice frame to my drawing."

Such a creative freedom can only be observed in adults when they are artists. I would see here the expression of a dream work: the black colour, indicating sadness and mourning, becomes here the container of the whole bright coloured drawing, expressing life drives. At high speed, the child integrates sadness to his experience of life, without abandoning the lively part of it. The same child noted on another occasion: "The teacher told us that black contains all the colours. That's why I like it". An analyst might see here an integrative movement of the depressive position.

Example six

The same boy gives the observer a drawing showing a character behind regular, thick, horizontal barrels. "Is he imprisoned?" asks the observer. "Oh no! He is climbing a ladder!" Like an image of a dream, we may note here the polymorphic quality of the drawing. A good capacity of reverie would be required to give back to the boy the quality of imprisonment that might be experienced in the "climbing" of ego development!

Example seven

The verbal commentaries made by the drawer may take part in putting the drawing at a secondary level of narration, under the condition that the observer/analyst would respect the odds and contradictions of the situation as a whole.

The same four-year-old boy is drawing and talking at the same time. "It is Mummy; 'bad ones' are throwing things at her". The drawing represents a human character, whose head is a window. Above her, more or less rectangular objects carefully coloured with bright, joyful colours. That is all. "And where are the bad ones?" the observer asks. "One can't see them, the sheet was cut; they are outside the sheet." Here, the "bad ones" are not represented, like in several examples of dream or of fears described above. The psychoanalyst has to respect both the splitting (the "cut sheet") and such a "shapeless representation". Here, the child is splitting his own parts that attack his mother. And because he has a fairly healthy development, he does not give a precise shape to those attacking parts. According to me, it is the landmark of a healthy way of functioning, because, contrary to a too rigid "figurability", a "shapeless representation" is ready for any psychic transformation to come.

Example eight

A ten-year-old boy is placed in a foster family because he had been mistreated and rejected by his mother, who then lost her parental rights to him. He regularly sees his father, his grandparents both paternal and maternal, but never his mother, who fails to take all the opportunities she is offered to meet her child.

When he is six or seven years old, his school asks for a psychiatric examination, because he is very aggressive and violent towards his schoolmates.

After different prescriptions, he is given a psychoanalytical psychotherapy once a week with a woman analyst when he is ten years old. There, he does not speak much, but makes many drawings on a repetitive pattern: he draws "bad Cyclopes", equipped with a single eye, plus lots of arms and several tails that throw venom on everybody that would dare approach one of them. The Cyclopes' enemies are "the human beings, because these are the bad ones".

In a session that takes place after eight months of treatment, he draws a Cyclopes with *two eyes*! Needless to say, he immediately scribbles them out and says he made a mistake. However, his behaviour at school is improving and he is becoming less frightened by emotional contact. Could the therapy have allowed him to rediscover the contact with the dreaming eyes of the mother and recover some elements of a "binocular vision" (Bion, 1962)?

Conclusion

In order to speak about dreams in children, I examined the child's verbal fantasies as well as his activities of playing and drawing. I did so from the point of view of the modern analytic way of considering dreaming and dream work (Meltzer, 1984). Beyond their apparent differences, I found it more fruitful to study their similarities and articulations.

It should be noted that the present chapter does not give hallucination and hallucinosis the place they deserve in the modern landscape of psychoanalysis, with the outstanding studies made about them (Bion, 1965). I would like to argue that, in the young child who is neither autistic nor severely psychotic, we do not encounter a hallucinatory organisation as we do in adults. The form of hallucination observed in my clinical material is the one Freud described in the "hallucinatory satisfaction of desire", not a pathological structured one.

Being part of an observation or of an analytic session with a young child requires the observer or the psychoanalyst to dive into a state of reverie. However, I maintain that the child also functions the same way if only we do not put on him an educative, realistic demand. A normal child is aware of external reality; there is no need to push it onto him as if he were a delusional person.

Melanie Klein (1929) considered that playing, for the young child, is equivalent to dreaming for the adult. She had understood that the same processes organise both activities, as long as they are considered as a dynamic process of unconscious psychic life.

René Diatkine (1994) considered that playing had a twofold function: expressing the transference situation while simultaneously denying its meaning. I would say the same about any dream narrative.

From a neurophysiologic point of view, it is now well known that the newborn—even the foetus—has a dream activity. In this chapter, we kept our investigation to the young child from two to six.

I hold that there is no need to centre and limit our attention to the child's narrative of his dreams of the night. Due to the fragility of their symbolisation tools, they will rarely give us an articulate narrative of a dream. In contrast, we shall have any opportunity to get narratives of their fantasy activity by observing the way they play, draw, and talk about these activities.

It is in the dynamics of an analytic session with such a young child that we shall observe at best his movements of inhibition, splitting, denial, regression, and so on. If we respect the way primary logics (Matte Blanco, 1975) works in the child's narrative, we shall be able to locate the conflicts between the realisation of desire and the psychic pain, as well as the means used by the child to either contain or avoid the situation. Any question about the narrative of a dream, a play, or a drawing will often bring about rationalisations, sometimes an additional meaningful detail, once in a while a possibility for the analyst to better understand the ego resistances of the young patient and to go one step further with him along the way of the analytic process.

Notes

1. I borrow that expression from the title of the film by J. C. Moutout, 2008.
2. In Latin, *in-fans* means "unable to speak".

References

Anzieu, A. (2004). *Le dessin de l'enfant, de l'approche génétique à l'interprétation*. Paris: Pensée Sauvage.

Bion, W. R. (1948). *Experiences in Groups*. London: Tavistock, 1961.

Bion, W. R. (1962). The psycho-analytic study of thinking. *International Journal of Psycho-analysis*, 43: 306–310.

Bion, W. R. (1965). *Transformations*. London: Heinemann.

Bion, W. R. (1970). *Attention and Interpretation*. London: Tavistock [reprinted London: Karnac, 1984].

Diatkine, R. (1994) *L'enfant dans l'adulte ou l'éternelle capacité de rêverie*. Lausanne: Delachaux & Niestlé.

Freud, A. (1927). *The Psycho-analytical Treatment of Children*. Oxford: Imago, 1946.

Freud, S. (1900a). *The Interpretation of Dreams*. S.E:, 4–5. London: Hogarth.

Freud, S. (1918b). *From the History of an Infantile Neurosis*. S. E., 17: 1–13. London: Hogarth.

Freud, S. (1919h). The 'uncanny'. S. E., 17: 217–252. London: Hogarth.

Freud, S. (1923b). *The Ego and the Id*. S. E., 19: 12–66. London: Hogarth.

Guignard, F. (1996). The Infantile in the analytical relationship, *International Journal of Psycho-analysis*, 76(6): 1083–1092.

Klein, M. (1923). The development of a child. *International Journal of Psycho-analysis*, 4: 419–474.

Klein, M. (1929). Personification in the play of children. *International Journal of Psycho-Analysis*, 10: 193–204.

Matte Blanco, I. (1975). *The Unconscious as Infinite Sets. An Essay in Bi-logic*. London: Duckworth.

Meltzer, D. (1984). *Dream-Life*. Aberdeen: Clunie.

Roussillon, R. (1995). La métapsychologie des processus et la transitionnalité. *Revue français de Psychanalyse, LIX*(spécial Congrès Paris, PUF): 1351–1522.
Winnicott, D. W. (1956). Primary maternal preoccupation. In: *Through Paediatrics to Psycho-Analysis. The Collected Papers of D. W. Winnicott* (pp. 300–305). London: Tavistock, 1975.
Winnicott, D. W. (1958). *Through Paediatrics to Psychoanalysis: The Collected Papers of D. W. Winnicott.* London: Tavistock, 1975.
Winnicott, D. W. (1971). *Jeu et Réalité. L'espace potentiel.* Paris: PUF, 1975.

CHAPTER FOUR

On not being able to dream: the role of maternal containment in the therapy of a young child who suffered from night terrors

Christine Anzieu-Premmereur

The French psychoanalyst, Jean Bertrand Pontalis (1972), wrote: "dreaming is first of all the effort to maintain an impossible union with the mother".

In his theory of the Skin Ego, *Le Moi-peau*, Didier Anzieu (1989) explored the way in which the infant's first experiences of being touched by the mother organises a container *in the relationship* for psychic functioning capable of providing a mental space in which representations and fantasies can be stored. If this maternal container is stable and flexible enough, an infant's early fears and anxieties are transformed into less violent experiences and can then be associated with dreams.

Wilfred Bion (1962) spoke of a "mental skin" that will allow the introjection of thinkable elements. But if archaic fears are too intense, they will block this process and so interfere with the infant's access to representations and symbolisations.

My work with young children has made me aware of their ability to create representations that give a sense of their early, disorganised experiences, and of how these have been integrated. The transference enables a process of representation and symbolisation, through play and through the exchange of feelings that can be taken in, contained, and processed during the session.

Reports of dreams are frequent in child analysis; you merely have to ask children while they are playing or drawing, "Like something in your bad dreams, is it?" Young children absorbed in their activities are very close to their preconscious and this makes it easy for them to talk about or demonstrate their dreams.

Primitive anxieties associated with defects in the maternal object are at the core of most analytic treatments with these children. Dreams help to show the connection with the object and to maintain a protection against the fear of an omnipotent maternal figure.

The capacity to dream and create representations that are sufficiently well-organised to be remembered is, however, linked to good emotional regulation and symbolisation. Some children never attain this ability because of a lack of containment of their disorganised and often traumatising experiences.

Peter

I shall now present the first sessions with Peter, who was five when I met him. He suffered from bouts of night terror; he was unable to sleep without acting out his fears, and he was an anorexic and depressed child.

In the analytic setting, a dream is an important representation that helps the analyst to capture the child's fantasies in the transference, and it can allow access to the preverbal and pre-symbolic experiences of early infancy.

Dreaming is a process of representation with a function of wish fulfilment, but it is also associated with traumatic experiences of pre-symbolic origin. Ferenczi's hypothesis (1931) was that dreams serve to recover memory traces of painful sensations. This possibility of working through experience, which Ferenczi called the traumatolytic function of dreams, is close to the idea of "healing dreams" in Winnicott's "Hate in the counter-transference" (1949).

In order to become communicable, emotions must go through a process of transformation and take on a symbolic form: emotional experiences are thus transformed and new connections are set up. In Bion's theory (1962), it is from dreams that the unconscious develops. Dreaming is seen as the most important component of the "psychoanalytic function of the personality". For Bion, a child is born with a rudimentary consciousness and senses stimuli, but is unaware of himself. Bion noted (1962), "The mother's capacity for reverie is the receptor organ for the infant's harvest of self-sensation gained by its conscious." Through her reverie, her ability to receive and transform the child's projective identifications, the mother expresses her love for the child, contains his anxieties, and provides him with the means of forming an alpha-function of his own based on the experience of being cared for by her.

What is important is the child's ability to create representations: that he can create representations and images out of sensations and perceptions, and can develop images of his relationship with his parents. The support and the holding that the mother provides for her baby ensure the continuity of his memory of sensations, pleasant or unpleasant. With the aid of her mirroring function, the mother returns his experiences to the child, transformed in a way that makes them feel "its own".

The capacity of the mother's unconscious to bind drives plays an important role in the child's ability to dream. If the mother, or the maternal care-giver, can empathise with the infant, if she can absorb his disorganised emotions and transform them, she will use her capacity for containment to calm the baby while at the same time stimulating its libido. There is a cohesive power in the maternal function, capable of maintaining the links between sensations, and this is a power that can neutralise the death instinct in the child's unconscious and thus stem the paranoid projections of his fears and aggression.

Peter, the child who could not dream

Peter was a five-year-old boy who had suffered from night terrors since he was a toddler. When he was eighteen months old, he would scream three or four times a night, breaking into a sweat, his eyes wide open, yet still asleep. He had no memory of these episodes, while his parents were unable to sleep and could never understand what was happening to him. They only consulted me when he was five because a friend had told them that there might be something psychological that could be treated. They were scared by their son's behaviour at night but never spoke to anybody about it. Were they ashamed of not being able to calm him?

Peter's mother had too heavy a workload to be able to look after him, but the father spent a great deal of his time at home with the children. He was an understanding man, and very aware of their anxieties and depressive feelings; at times he would cry when talking about them, while the mother looked at him with a slight smile as if doubting his feelings. But he was not the kind of person to cuddle the boy and give him a sense of warmth and protection; he was a muscular, masculine man, uncomfortable with physical contact.

The mother reported that at Peter's birth, she found herself unable to take him in her arms. He was born after an emergency caesarean section, and she had felt disconnected from the birth. She said she could not feel what other women had reported, the intense feeling of love and tenderness for the new-born baby. She had only felt great distress. She had no memory of Peter's early months, everything was "normal", she said, trying to avoid memories of the post partum and of Peter's early childhood. He grew without needing her attention; that was easy. She went back to work two months after the birth and he did not preoccupy her.

In response to my doubts over this account, the father remembered her being in a panic at the idea of being alone with the baby, who screamed day and night "like an animal". She could hardly bring herself to touch him and she was only able to breast-feed when her own mother came and looked after her in her distress.

She was shocked when, at twelve months, Peter started to have problems sleeping. He refused to sleep alone in his room. He did not have any form of transitional object but finally settled down when sucking a dummy. But when he was two, his parents decided to throw his dummies in the bin, afraid that he might become addicted to such infantile objects, and told him that a mysterious man had taken them. The night terrors, which had started when he was eighteen months old then intensified, accompanied by a fear of a phantom presence in the room and by the invention of an imaginary friend. The parents found this very disturbing, but they did not like to ask for help, so they did not talk about it to the paediatrician.

They finally came to me when he was five because they were exhausted and overwhelmed by the problem.

From the day I met them for this first consultation and asked them to tell me in detail about Peter's infancy and their own feelings, his symptoms disappeared. They showed no surprise that Peter's sleep disorder disappeared before I had even met him. The parents were simply very happy and relieved, and seemed to have a very positive attitude towards me, though this was accompanied by a perceptible ambivalence in the mother: she could not see why she should bring her son to the sessions herself. She thought that the father or the babysitter could do this job: it had nothing to do with her. For her, being a mother meant giving birth and being responsible for her child, but it did not mean doing anything specific for him. Anyone could fulfill the child's needs; she simply could not see that her presence as the mother was important to him (and to me). Taking care of her as a mother in despair and of the father as an infantile, regressive person, I became a maternal container for both of them. They were relieved that I did not pass judgement on them as bad parents and that I had not been frightened off by their fears.

On waking, Peter had no awareness of the night terrors. He felt that he had slept through the night. Actually he had always been very restless as a baby during the night, tossing and turning and frequently crying out, as if he were never completely asleep. The father even thought, judging by his son's restlessness during the night, that he never in fact had dreams. He also noticed that his son could not wake up without crying in the morning or after a nap. The mother felt this was normal since it had also happened to her. Non-integrated parts of the personality, as Bion reminds us, raw sensory data, and beta elements, may result in a state in which the child does not know whether he is awake or dreaming. I think Peter did not so much produce dreams as experience an accumulation of concrete elements that occupied his mental–emotional inner space and acquired a terrifying character so that he was unable to dream and could not even wake up. These undigested beta elements were not transformed by any alpha function, and therefore could not become part of a dream.

Peter seemed to nourish a hope of finding someone who might help him work through the experiences that frightened him. The atmosphere in his sessions was full of tension and despair, and I had the impression he was stuck in situations dominated by primitive fears.

In the first meeting with Peter and his mother he was very upset that his mother talked about him and about how she experienced his screaming at night. Since he was not aware of the night terrors this narrative made him feel depersonalised. He said he hated it when his mother talked about a part of him he did not know anything about; he said he felt as if he were being cut into tiny pieces and they were falling down around him. To counter this sense of disorganisation, he asked her if she remembered moments when they had had fun together, like reading his best book, or watching his favourite movie. He was trying to make up for the scary experience of not recognising himself in her account of his night terrors. In this search for the pleasures he had shared with her lay a sign of his hope that he might be healed. But she did not have any memory of these happier experiences. He tried to give her clues, mentioning books or scenes from movies and walks they had gone on together, but she was distracted and could not pay attention to him. The child's needs irritated her and she started complaining, saying she could not understand how he could be so infantile—asking about anything so unimportant.

It was painful for her to pay much attention to him and when he asked her for a snack, she realised that she had forgotten to bring him any food for after school; her bag was empty, as she was herself. She told him to be quiet and to stop using my toys, implying he was being very rude to use part of my room to play in. She said he was being too noisy and she did not like it when he tried to get her attention in such a babyish manner. Peter looked sad, and after one or two provocative attempts to get her attention, he switched to talking about his success at school. That was the only way for him to get a positive reaction from her. I realised then how much her narcissism had been wounded by this child. I commented on how difficult it was for them to feel comfortable together, and how lonely they must feel, even if they were together in one room. Surprisingly this made her think of Peter's defence against loneliness: his imaginary companion, a ghost that never left him on his own.

In Peter's first session alone he immediately wanted to draw this ghost. It was a presence you could not touch and was always quietly behind him. He could not live without it. But sometimes this ghost was frightening. And Peter had to look behind him many times to be sure there was no danger there. I said "You must be afraid of being alone with me as I am a stranger and this is an unknown room." Then he made a drawing. He complained that my black pens were not dark enough to represent The Fear. While he was drawing, doing it carefully and with his full attention on it, he said that something weird had happened to him, that for the first time in his life he had had a dream.

He did not know what it was but when he woke up he remembered a vague shape around him. Anxiously, he had reported this new experience to his father who congratulated him on no longer having night terrors. His father explained to him that he had dreamt, that this was what we called a dream, these night experiences with pictures that we can remember. Peter was proud that he had learned something so important, that he had learned the word "dream" and the fact that at night we have pictures in our minds. The transference was immediately powerful.

Winnicott (1949) wrote:

> Dreams play a central part in the process of the working through of emotional experiences. When dream work fails in performing this function, the capacity to form symbols is affected. I think there is not necessarily an integration between a child asleep and a child awake. This integration comes in the course of time. Once dreams are remembered and even conveyed somehow to a third person, the dissociation is broken down a little; but some people never clearly remember their dreams, and children depend very much on adults for getting to know their dreams. It is normal for small children to have anxiety dreams and terrors. At these times children need someone to help them to remember what they dreamed. It is a valuable experience whenever a dream is both dreamed *and* remembered, precisely because of the breakdown of dissociation that this represents.

After this session Peter asked patients in the waiting room if they also needed my help with their dreams. And he asked me in each succeeding session if I saw other children in my office, saying he was sure he was the only one to see me. He was always careful to tell me any dream he had and was sad when he did not have any between sessions.

So, slowly, during this first session, he drew a long, continuous, very wavy line all around the page. The waves finally reached the centre of the page; the impression was of something grey and sad. I commented that these shapes must be very important to him and said that I felt it had to do with a sad feeling. He then added eyes, making it into a picture of two snakes and suddenly added a full circle all around the drawing. I said, "It must make you feel good to be wrapped up so safely". He nodded in agreement, and I added that it is a good feeling to have a ghost that never leaves you all on your own.

He had never thought of it like that, he said, and he decided to reorganise the drawing, splitting the page into two parts, one for the bad ghost with a mouth, and one for the not-bad one with ears and eyes. Since in French the word for eyes is *yeux* and my name is Anzieu, I said "like Anzieu who listens to you". This instantly made him think of the round shells he had brought back from the beach in the summer, and of how I had told him he could hear the sound of the sea if he put one close up to his ear. As sea is *la mer* in French, which sounds exactly like *la mère*, the mother, he understood what I meant. "Yes", he said, "like the music that makes me think of her", and he sang a nursery rhyme that helped him to think of his Mummy; he said that it helped him remember her better than sweets because she never gave him sugar, but that he did not have much appetite anyway.

In effect, we were playing with representations of the good breast, and with how to cope with the absence of his mother. The world of drives, of pleasure, and of frustration, was alive again.

And so our framework was also important for containment and providing a transitional space for the analytical relationship. Peter was angry with me when I told him he could not take his drawings home: they were to stay in a file in my closet. Choosing the right colour, green, for his file, and writing his name, the same last name as Daddy, was important. Then he carefully checked that the lock on my cupboard was secure and offered me a compromise: I could keep the file safe, but he would have the right to have my card with my name on it and to keep it in his pocket when he was out of my office.

In the next sessions he talked about the ghost as if I already knew his mind; we had developed a real complicity and had a good laugh together. At the end of a session, he had to come back many times to knock at my door and say goodbye again to be sure that I was not dead. He complained of nightmares in which ghosts were trying to eat him. The ghost characters became more libidinal and less shapeless, the pattern of change in his dreams became more and more about fighting against maternal intrusion and incestuous wishes. He found a green container in my room that he labelled the green monster and this was there to swallow the nightmares: it was "the biggest mouth in the world" and I was to keep a eye on it while he was away. He also reported being afraid of shadows in my office that reminded him of "weird objects" he had been afraid of as a baby.

This reminded me of Bertram Lewin (1946):

> The dream screen appears to represent the breast during sleep, but it is ordinarily obscured by the various derivatives of the preconscious and unconscious that locate themselves before it or upon it. These derivatives, according to Freud, are the intruders in sleep. They threaten to wake us up, and it is them in disguise that we see as the visual contents of the dream. (pp. 419–434)

And further:

> That ego boundaries are lost in sleep and dreams we know thanks to Federn's classic paper. I should like to utilize Federn's discovery to support my contention that the dreamer, or sleeper, remains in unified contact with the breast and that this determines the constant characteristics of the dream, such as the dream screen, which are not always readily noted. (p. 420)

After only a few sessions the ghosts disappeared, and I learned from the parents that Peter had stopped suffering from the eczema and the allergies that he had had for three years and that they had forgotten to tell me about.

As to dealing with saying goodbye, Peter found a way to do this without too much anxiety or sadness by taking a round piece of play-dough he had made during a session and keeping it in his hand. I agreed to his taking this home on condition that he brought it back. He never forgot and started to go to sleep with the ball in his hands. He named the play dough "the dough of dreams" (*la pâte à rêves*), telling me that I was lucky because he was sure I was able to make my own dreams with this brightly coloured play dough.

His dreams were peopled with frightening beings without any real shape, and with ghosts or weird dragons, either too shadowy or too agitating. The first dream that was not about a ghost, two weeks after the beginning of our analysis, showed the integration of a maternal container and the assertiveness of a stronger ego: "I am building a house with other people".

The next dreams were much more phallic, dealing with an excitement difficult to contain: "a rocket leaving earth to go to the moon, with a lot of fire". And his new sense of guilt made him tell how often he was dreaming of finding ways "to repair the silly things he had done at home".

This sad little inhibited, anorexic boy became a hungry, masculine soccer player, able to get happily excited. Libidinal life had returned, as his dreams became more and more oedipal.

The night terrors came back during the summer break that interrupted the sessions for six weeks. He had been with his family, excited by the company of his cousins and all the physical activity, all the running about and jumping into water. As soon as his parents left him with the grandparents the night terrors and moments of sleepwalking reappeared, showing how very vulnerable his psyche still was.

Peter came back many years after the end of his psychoanalysis to talk about some school problems. He said he remembered very well that I was the only one who knew about the difference between ghosts and dreams.

He asked me "Do you still have the dog?" In his imagination and reconstruction of our sessions I always had a dear little, soft, white dog asleep at my feet: a beautiful condensation of the contained drives and the recovery of a sensual encounter with a maternal figure in the transference.

The search for a friend in the analytic field corresponds to the need to meet a reliable, supportive, and complementary other. At times in the analysis we would look at ourselves in the mirror and he saw resemblances between us—in the eyebrow or in the way the hair grew. This game of seeing in me a double of himself was reassuring. It helped to balance the disquieting strangeness of the phantom and gave narcissistic support.

Dreams help the analyst to understand the process of mastering drives. Sexuality is rooted in early bodily sensations, in the tender exchanges between mother and child, and also in the early fantasies stimulated by the primal scene. These early sexual experiences cannot be assimilated. Laplanche (1997) argues that sexuality and attendant fears take shape in the human mind through the traces of the child's encounters with adult sexuality. These inevitable encounters are over-stimulating, confusing, and traumatic, "a confusion of tongues", in Ferenczi's term (1931).

With an immature ego, Peter had difficulties coping with his paranoid fears and his sexual excitement, his fear of threatening disorganisation, and his confusion when faced with loss and separation.

In his paper on sleep (1938) Otto Isakower wrote:

> When we fall asleep, the ego withdraws its interest and its cathexes from the external world. We know that they are not cut off at a single blow, but that the process is a gradual one: as sleep comes upon us, the world does not vanish suddenly and totally. With the alteration in

the distribution of cathexis between ego and external world it is, however, inevitable that some change should take place in the ego, and this change I believe to be principally characterized by two processes: (1) a disintegration of the various parts and functions of the ego; and (2) a diminution of the ego's differentiations. This latter process seems to set in somewhat later than the dissociation of the parts and functions of the ego.

Dreaming requires a capacity for figuration that is based on the body sensations, and visual and auditory perceptions contained and organised by the mother and associated with primitive, pleasurable experiences. But there is also a function of the discharge of arousals in dreams, as Bion showed. The non-representable parts of the primitive experience, which cannot be put into words, are communicated to the analyst through projective identification, and the analyst's role is to contain and transform them. When this happens the dreamer has, in effect, evacuated the "weird objects" of his archaic fears and lodged them in the analyst.

The experience of talking about a dream and having it understood and interpreted fills the self with a sense of its own existence. Dreaming and reporting a dream to a good, attentive listener has something of a transitional function. Dream space can be compared to transitional space. The analytic setting, the dynamics in the play space, and the transformations experienced in the meeting with the analyst, enable the child to set up a transitional space that had been lacking or was insufficient in the past. Peter twice had the new experience of a transitional space, first when his parents became able to contain their own anxieties and conflicts after the first session, and again when he met me and discovered a playful relationship. Before that, he had acted out his unconscious experiences at night in his parents' space.

In his study of the maternal function in calming the baby, the French analyst, Michel Fain (1971) wrote that the function of acting as a protective shield can be carried out in different ways by the mother: as a pragmatic, calming manoeuvre to get the child to go to sleep without providing it with satisfaction, or as a complex message by which she conveys both satisfaction and calming. This will have complex effects on the baby's ability to create representations.

Night terrors are not dreams. They point to what is missing and thus to what it takes for a person to be able to dream. The child builds his own capacity for representation by introjecting the maternal presence, so containing its own disorganised fears, and also by having her as the first one to listen to his report of the experience of the night.

Certain traumatic experiences can make the dream process unavailable to the child for a while, and in this case it will again be exposed to archaic fears, and again be overwhelmed by the stimulation and discharge of its drives.

Identification with a secure mother is helpful, for it means the child has a representation of her when she is absent or when in the child's mind going to sleep becomes too closely connected with a sensation of dying.

Night terrors do *not take place in sleep*, though they are initiated out of it, but in a dissociated state characterised by a waking alpha rhythm during which the subject is disoriented and may be delusional or hallucinating. Stage four arousals are associated with all degrees of anxiety, only about one third attaining night terror proportions. More than two thirds of all night terrors take place during the first non-rapid eye movement (NREM) period. In its fully developed form, the night terror combines somnambulism, sleep-talking, and anxiety of panic intensity. There is often complete amnesia for the episode, but varying degrees of recovery of content can take place, generally consisting of a single terrifying event.

References

Anzieu, D. (1989). *The Skin Ego, a Psychoanalytic Approach to the Self*. Newhaven, CT: Yale University Press.

Bion, W. R. (1962). The psycho-analytic study of thinking. *International Journal of Psycho-analysis, 43*: 306–310.

Fain, M. (1971). The prelude to fantasmatic life. In: D. Birksted-Breen, S. Flanders, & A. Gibeault (Eds.), *Reading French Psychoanalysis*. London & New York: Routledge, 2010.

Ferenczi, S. (1931). On the revision of the interpretation of dreams. In: *Notes and Fragments. Final Contributions to the Problems and Methods of Psycho-analysis* (pp. 238–243). London: Hogarth, 1955 [reprinted London: Karnac, 1980].

Isakower, O. (1938). A contribution to the patho-psychology of phenomena associated with falling asleep. *International Journal Psycho-Analysis, 19*: 331–345.

Laplanche, J. (1997). The theory of seduction and the problem of the other. *International Journal of Psycho-Analysis, 78*: 653–666.

Lewin, B. D. (1946). Sleep, the mouth, and the dream screen. *The Psychoanalytic Quarterly, 15*: 419–434.

Pontalis, J. B. (1972). La pénétration du rêve. *Nouvelle Revue de Psychanalyse, 5*: 257–271.

Winnicott, D. W. (1949). Hate in the counter-transference. *International Journal of Psycho-Analysis, 30*: 69–74.

CHAPTER FIVE

Dream, phantasy, and children's play: Spaces in which a child approaches thinking between wish-fulfilment, mental processing of affect, and mastering of reality

Michael Günter

It is relatively rare for children to recount their dreams. If they do, then their accounts, at least in very young children, are often very short and mostly followed by the urgent demand not to waste time, please, but to get on with playing. Associations are not forthcoming, and anyway the dreams of very young children are often quite easy to understand. Perhaps this is overstating the case and dismissing the subject too briefly. In individual cases, and above all with adolescents, it is certainly possible to work with (and on) dreams just as we do with adults. Nevertheless the view outlines certain peculiarities of children's thinking which had already been observed early on in psychoanalysis.

Freud's depiction of children's dreams

In the eighth of his lectures in the *Introductory Lectures on Psychoanalysis*, Freud tried to convey the two main characteristics of dreams to his listeners and readers as clearly as possible, and because dream-distortion makes understanding dreams much harder, it seemed best to avoid this at first "by keeping to dreams in which there was no distortion or only a very little" (1916-1917, p. 126) and continued:

> The dreams we are in search of occur in children. They are short, clear, coherent, easy to understand and unambiguous; but they are nevertheless undoubtedly dreams. You must not suppose, however, that all children's dreams are of this kind. Dream-distortion sets in very early in childhood, and dreams dreamt by children of between five and eight have been reported which bear all the characteristics of later ones. But if you limit yourselves to ages between the beginning of observable mental activity and the fourth or fifth year, you will come upon a number of dreams which possess the characteristics that can be described as "infantile" and you will find a few of the same kind in later years of childhood. Indeed, under certain conditions even adults have dreams which are quite similar to the typically infantile ones. (p. 126)

As is well known, his reflections led Freud to the conviction that the stimulus for dreaming lay in a wish, and that the fulfilment of this wish formed the content of the dream. The second characteristic Freud noted and described was that the dream presented the wish as fulfilled in a hallucinatory experience. And beyond wish-fulfilment he saw "the transformation of a thought into an experience" (p. 129) as an equally central quality of dreaming. It was also from his intensive study of children's dreams that he deduced the essential function of dreams, stating that dreams were the guardians of sleep. Given the character of these infantile and thus easily comprehensible dreams, Freud continued, one had no need to use free association or explore the unconscious. As a result there was no need to turn to the techniques of psychoanalysis to decipher the manifest dream that so clearly matched the latent dream thought.

Finding my initial unease with the topic supported by so high an authority, I could declare the task assigned to me to be largely completed and quietly put down my pen. I shall, however, despite the apparent simplicity and unrewarding character of children's dreams, offer some thoughts on the subject presenting my own view of children's dreams and play for discussion.

In this eighth lecture Freud pointed out further important features: one was his designation of children's dreams as "intelligible, completely valid mental acts" (p. 127). He further stated that a child's dream was a reaction to an experience from the previous day that had left behind it a wish that had not been dealt with. The dreamer "would rather continue his work on the things he is concerned with and for that reason he does not fall asleep" (p. 128). So dreaming was often a reaction to psychical sleep-disturbing stimuli. And a little further on: "In so far as a dream is a reaction to a psychical stimulus it must be equivalent to dealing with the stimulus in such a way that it is got rid of and that sleep can continue" (p. 129). The dream removes the stimulus, does away with it, deals with it through a form of experience. In this eighth lecture, Freud moves away from the concept of regression in dreams that he had developed in the *The Interpretation of Dreams* and introduces here the beginnings of a concept of dreaming as a psychical procedure for the processing of stimuli. Without explicitly setting it out as such, in the *Lectures*, written twenty-five years after the *The Interpretation of Dreams*, Freud in fact formulated approaches to a concept of dreaming as a *thinking* process. And it is a shift of accent of this kind towards an understanding of dreaming as a process of thinking under the specific, regression-conducive conditions of sleep, that largely characterises the present-day psychoanalytical perception of dreams.[1]

Psychoanalytic developmental psychology of dreaming

But let us first of all take a further look at the question of the developmental psychology of dreaming touched on above: in this volume Elizabeth Brainin relates the development of dreams to the ego development in children (see Brainin, Chapter One, pp. 1–21). In particular, the mechanisms of condensation, displacement, or reversal to the opposite, symbolisation, and distortion, which Freud described in *The Interpretation of Dreams*, only develop gradually so that, as Brainin writes, it is largely agreed that dream distortion in its full sense does not appear until around the age of five with the onset of the oedipal conflict (p. 11). The conflicts that are worked on in dreams are current developmental conflicts issuing from ego and superego development. Brainin emphasises in this connection that in contrast to adults, the content of whose dreams arises from both the past and the present, in very young children past and present are experienced as one entity. Psychoanalytical work with children's dreams, as she points out, is hampered by a further difficulty: the dreamlike state that is produced by the recounting of dreams is experienced by the children as regressive and is therefore warded off, with the result that it is just as difficult working with dreams as it is with free association.

Grotjahn had already noted in 1938 that children seldom reported their dreams spontaneously because:

> The healthy child with all its longing for pleasure is attached to the very thrilling present and is directed by the pleasure principle towards the future and therefore seldom spontaneously reports about the past. When it awakens the night is gone, is nothing; the need for a new day and new ventures inhibits every tendency to look back. Interest in the past is a very unchildlike attitude and is much more characteristic of the adult. (p. 507)

And he added that young children are very suggestible so that the material gained by asking questions could hardly be regarded as reliable. I should like to add that although their dreams are largely comparable to those of adults in their complexity and characteristic mechanisms, adolescents, too, are often extremely reluctant to talk about their dreams because at their still precarious stage of development they fear and try to avoid the regressive undertow that accompanies any telling of dreams.

Children's dreams as ways of thinking and of processing affects

One of the most impressive collections of a young child's dreams can be found in a work by Niederland published in 1957. In his essay "The earliest dreams of a young child", Niederland described and discussed eleven dreams that Johnny had between the ages of one year and five months and three years and eleven months. The dreams were recounted to him by Johnny's mother who was in analysis with Niederland. The sequence of these dreams provides a vivid picture of the development of children's dreams, as Elizabeth Brainin has illustrated in exemplary fashion, noting the relatively *late* development of the mechanisms of dream-work, that is, the complex operations of defence in dreams. However, when one examines the dreams as recounted by Johnny's mother in greater detail, evidence emerges that at an *early* stage the dreams of young children already contain elements showing engagement with conflicts and attempts to solve them.

However simply they may be structured, children's dreams, too, are essentially made up of psychical operations of thinking and affect processing. In other words, already in the dreams of young children an α-function in the sense of a processing of affects and sense data, of β-elements, takes effect. I should like to illustrate this with two of little Johnny's eleven dreams: the first two dreams when he was one year and five months old, and one year and eight months, could only be deduced from his behaviour and he did not report them. Here is how Niederland described the second one:

> Johnny experienced the next dream when he was twenty months old. It also was a nightmare and nonverbal. At that time his mother was in the seventh month of pregnancy with the second child. Johnny awoke during the night screaming wildly. When his mother entered his bedroom (where he slept alone), she found him standing in his crib, pressing his right fist tightly against his teeth. After being held for a little while in his mother's arms, he calmed down and fell asleep again. During the preceding day, according to the mother's account, about seven or eight hours before what may be presumed to have been a nightmare, his mother had been playing with him, whirling him about in her arms and holding him against her body. The mother considered it likely that he might have felt fetal movements in her abdomen. While the correctness of this idea cannot be ascertained, it was quite apparent that the child thoroughly enjoyed this game with his mother, when suddenly and vigorously he bit her nipple through the clothing. He had never done this before. The mother's pain was so intense that she slapped him and instantly put him down. She, too, had never done this before. Johnny cried, and may have become aware of the acute pain (or, at least, abrupt change in the mother's behavior) produced by his biting. That night he awoke screaming and holding his fist in his mouth, pressing it against his teeth—something not observed in him before. (Niederland, 1957, p. 191)

Although we have no record of what the little boy said, and therefore the interpretation has to remain to a certain degree speculative, I am inclined to believe that Johnny not only, as Brainin inferred, relived the traumatic scene of the previous day, but that beyond that he was thinking of possible solutions to it. I understand the fist held against his mouth as a condensed scenic representation of both biting, including the pleasure in biting, and also of the attempt to prevent himself from biting by putting his fist into his mouth and pressing it against his teeth. Possibly there was also an aspect of punishment there. What I see as important however is that Johnny's fear, which had gripped him during the night, led to an attempt to master the situation himself. So it triggered a processing of the affect in the sense of an α-function which then found expression in the scene depicted.

I shall pass over a few dreams and report the eighth, when Johnny was three years and three months old. One can see the enormous development not only in the language ability needed to report dreams, but also in the complex shaping of the manifest dream, in the dreamwork and presumably in the thinking processes within the dream.

> Two weeks after the baby's arrival [the mother gave birth to a third child] Johnny reported his next dream, which he had had while sleeping at his grandmother's house, where he slept in the latter's bedroom. During the night he suddenly awoke and shouted: "A parakeet bit me in my hand." He pointed to the back of his right hand between the thumb and index finger and urgently demanded to be allowed to sleep "with grandma in her bed." This was granted and the child soon fell asleep again. The dream was so vivid that on his awakening in the morning when he saw his grandmother in the other bed (where he had originally slept), Johnny exclaimed: "Get out of the bed, grandma! There is a parakeet in the bed. He will bite you!" He then explained in vivid detail that "the parakeet flew out of the tunnel zoo from the cage where the sea lions are. The parakeet flew first to my house. He did not find me in my house, because I slept in grandma's house. The parakeet then flew all the way to grandma's house into my bed and bit me in my hand. He came in through the window." (Niederland, 1957, pp. 194–195)

Niederland explained that Johnny often visited the zoo and showed great interest in the sea-lions. The parrot cage was close to where the sea-lions were kept, and Johnny noticed the parrots on one occasion because they were squawking loudly and beating their wings. When his younger brother was born, for several months Johnny showed great interest in a parrot which was kept in a cage next door to where he lived. When his mother took him and Charlie for a walk he always insisted on going to see this parrot. Once he saw several parrots in the cage and this preoccupied him. He kept asking where they came from. On the day before the parrot dream he had taken over Charlie's push-chair and kept saying he was a small baby or that he was called Charlie (Niederland, 1957, p. 194). The close connection of the dream with the arrival of the next sibling is clear. Even if we do not have access to the child's associations, the background described is sufficient to make these links between Johnny's thinking and his experiences seem plausible. The threat posed by the baby brother is impressively represented by the parrot coming out of a tunnel like the baby brother.

What is striking in the complexity of thought processes here is the way he deals with the fact that the parrot first of all looks for him in his own house but does not find him there because he is sleeping at his grandmother's. Little Johnny's first line of defence against the threat fails for the parrot pursues him all the way to his grandmother's house. The dream's graphic representation corresponds exactly to Johnny's inner world. He was naturally unable to get rid of his thoughts that were constantly circling around the birth of the little brother and of the threat that this meant to his position. There was also no way to rid himself of the conflicts connected with the aggressive thoughts he harboured about the little intruder—despite the real distance from home that he had while staying with his grandmother. There the parrot finds him and bites him at a point exactly between the first and second finger. One can assume this dream idea is a complex, highly condensed visual manifestation of several conflicting thoughts. We can only speculate on the underlying elements contained in this dream idea, since the specific individual meaning could only be confirmed through associations. I am convinced that this image owes its emergence to a complex mental process. One could for instance speculate that the place where the parrot bit him, exactly between the first and second finger, represents Johnny's conscious and unconscious preoccupation with the wish to be the first and only child of his parents and the resulting feelings of guilt and the desire to punish himself.

Though children's dreams too, presumably from the beginning of the child's capacity to think, are to be regarded as a thinking process and more specifically as problem-solving thinking, this form of thinking still requires time to reach a certain level of complexity. One can regard the emergence of complexity, as described above, as related to ego development, and show from this perspective how the mechanisms of dream-work that Freud described only develop gradually, thus producing dreams of more complex form.

One can also describe this development from the viewpoint of object relations psychology. Anzieu-Premmereur (see Chapter Four, pp. 65–66) has suggested an understanding of children's dreams whereby the child gradually introjects the maternal presence and her reverie, and in this way acquires his own dreamlike imaginative powers. The child is seen as becoming capable via this introjection of developing dreams in the stricter sense and of processing affects in his sleep with their aid. Such dreams thus stand in contrast to simple anxiety dreams. One could say that the child gradually internalises the mother' ability to process β-elements in her reverie, and with it the corresponding mode of relating. This internalisation of the mother's α-function is reflected in the increasingly differentiated organisation of the child's dreams.

Children's play as an analogy to dreaming

Besides the fact that children's dreams as mentioned earlier on are simple in structure, and also besides the fact of their aversion to the kind of reflection that encourages regression, there is yet another reason why concerning oneself with children's dreams can at times seem relatively unproductive. Children throw themselves into whatever is going on, that is, into here-and-now play activities with the analyst. Here they can develop their fantasies far more broadly and above all can *act* them out. This is far more satisfying to them than analysing a dream that is already half forgotten. Adolescents, too, tend to show a certain reserve over reflecting on night dreams because the events that take place in them appear somewhat out of their control. Such loss of control is likely to threaten adolescents with the destabilisation of their precarious ego-functions.

However, the children's world of fantasy and play fully compensates for the lack of available dreams to work on in analysis. In his work "Playing: its theoretical status in the clinical situation", Winnicott wrote "In playing, the child manipulates external phenomena in the service of the dream and invests chosen external phenomena with dream meaning and feeling" (1968, p. 598). Freud had already (1916–1917, p. 376) spoken of art as "the half-way region of phantasy", and pointed out the parallel qualities of thought processes in dreaming, in the world of phantasy, in children's play, and in art. He saw these areas as having in common that they represented "the fulfilment of a wish, a correction of unsatisfying reality" (1908e, p. 146).

The process of thinking in images, children's play, and artwork all offer us the possibility of turning away from reality and of finding satisfaction in illusions (Freud, 1930a). Admittedly, in play the spell of the hallucinatory quality of wish-fulfilment in dreaming is broken through the player's proximity to reality and is therefore relativised. This position of play as lying "in between", "in a half-way region", in a transitional space as Winnicott formulated it, and the accompanying fantasies the child creates make both play and fantasy useful in therapy, just as precisely this intermediary position of a child's play between inner world and outer world gives playing its central function for certain developmental processes in the child.

Interestingly, the broad equation of children's play with the dreams of adults is borne out by results in neurobiological research: Koukkou and Lehmann assume in their "functional state-shift model" (1980, 1983) that in sleep "fluctuations of the functional brain state" appear (2000), or more exactly that in neurophysiological terms there is a "functional regression of the organisational level of neuronal networks during sleep" (2000, p. 241). The "recurring physiological regressions of the functional brain state towards childhood during sleep (sleep phases) serve the functions of sleep and are the basis of the processes through which dreaming emerges" (p. 241). Thus an activation of memory representations on the lowest level of complexity occurs, as is characteristic of children's thinking. Dream thinking in sleep makes use of "the cognitive-emotional strategies of childhood" and this makes it possible for "new associations also of recent memories to be seen and treated in the same lordly manner as a child deals with its fantasies and realities in the waking state" (Koukkou & Lehmann 2000, p. 242).

This explains, as they see it, the characteristics of dreams that are closely related to children's thinking. In dreams, memory representations at a low level of complexity are reactivated. These are not accessible to waking thought with its higher level of complexity (cf. also von Klitzing, Chapter Seven, pp. 110–111). The memory structures and thinking strategies of an adult dreamer are thus similar to those of children in a waking state of consciousness. Looked at it the other way round, one can assume that children's thinking when they are awake, in particular when they are playing or fantasising, is close to dream thinking, and this is precisely what we experience in clinical work with children.

Freud reflected on the psychical functions of children's play in *Beyond the Pleasure Principle* (1920g) in the famous example of his grandchild's game with the cotton reel.

> The child had a wooden reel with a piece of string wound round it. It never occurred to him, for example, to drag this after him on the floor and so play horse and cart with it, but he kept throwing it with considerable skill, held by the string, over the side of his little draped cot, so that the reel disappeared into it, then said his significant "o-o-o-oh" and drew the reel by the string out of the cot again, greeting its reappearance with a joyful "*Da*" (there). This was therefore the complete game, disappearance and return, the first act being the only one generally observed by the onlookers, and the one untiringly repeated by the child as a game for its own sake, although the greater pleasure unquestionably attached to the second act. (Freud, 1920g, p. 15)

He interpreted this game as the expression of a major cultural achievement of the child, the renunciation of drive satisfaction: the child refrained from making a fuss when his mother went out to the theatre. Instead it set up its own performance with the disappearance and return of the cotton reel thus turning its passive position of exposure into an activity of its own. However, in discussing this further Freud at the same time emphasised that beyond the pleasure principle there was the compulsion to repeat. He saw this, alongside the pleasure principle, as the stimulus for the child's game. Thus one can say that playing this game serves the fulfilment of a wish as much as it seems to be dominated by the compulsion to repeat. Beyond that it represents an achievement in the child's active mastering of a traumatic situation: consequently playing represents a thinking process. It enables the child not only to represent and express its inner life but it also opens up spaces in which to act and think. With the help of play the child can grasp the situation it has experienced and process the affects that are part of it.

That is not all: by entering the intermediary space of play—that is to say the space in which inner states are depicted by means of external objects—and despite the fact that in play the child luckily still feels objects can be manipulated in a magically omnipotent way, he gradually develops the ability to distinguish between inner and outer worlds, and to accept the limitations that the external world imposes on its magical–omnipotent fantasies. In playing, the child can let itself go in his wishful fantasies and yet he knows at the same time that this is play and not in fact reality. He can move from one world to the other with what Reinhard Lempp referred to, in a rather neat term, as "the ability to climb over" (*Überstiegsfähigkeit* in the German original,

Lempp, 1984, 1991) a quality that he saw as central for integration into social reality. In psychoanalytic literature this is now referred to as "pretend mode", the term Fonagy introduced (Fonagy et al., 2002).

In the following two case vignettes I will now go on to present some thoughts of mine on the extent to which one can compare both the fantasies children develop and their play with dreams. The vignettes are both taken from interviews with children that I saw in a Therapeutic Care Home when they were being admitted or discharged. The Squiggle Game, developed by Winnicott, in which the child and the analyst take it in turns to make a squiggle on the paper and then let the other one turn it into something, made it easier for me to set up playful interaction with the children, and it also offers you as the reader a chance to follow the conversation in visual terms. It is easy to see how dreamlike many of the pictures and stories we developed from them are.

The world of dice and the world of people[2]

Mark, eight, was presented to me when he was admitted to a Therapeutic Care Home on leaving a foster family. As a result of his behaviour he had become very much an outsider in this family. I knew from a report on his background that his biological parents were both drug addicts. The father had died of an overdose of heroin, and his mother spent many years in prison for drug-related crime. Mark and his older sister showed the signs of years of neglect in the form of a deprivation syndrome and disorganised attachment style. He was prone to wolfing his food uncontrollably, had outbursts of aggression, and was extremely restless. Additional symptoms were encopresis and smearing of faeces, and also a language development disorder with agrammatism. Mark also had difficulties at school; he had problems with arithmetic and was retarded in motor skills and visuomotor perception (F 81.2, F 82) so that in earlier examinations there had been a question as to whether he might have an organic brain psychosyndrome. Two tests for cognitive ability produced disparate results: an IQ of 82 in CFT1, but an IQ of 97 in K-ABC.

After a few introductory remarks, I suggested to Mark that we should play the squiggle game, and he made my squiggle into a house with a path and a garage (Figure 1).

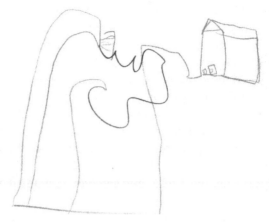

Figure 1. Squiggle game with Mark: a house with path and garage.

It was as if he was looking through a tangle of winding paths for a home to go to and be able to stay in. This was done, as it were, twice over, with the garage being a second attempt. You could say that the two buildings, though they are not so easy to identify in the picture, represented the Therapeutic Care Home where he currently was living and the foster family. When it was my turn I turned his squiggle into a castle (Figure 2), identifying (myself) with his wish for a really solid home, a safe place for him.

Figure 2. Squiggle game with Mark: a castle.

His reaction was to turn my next squiggle in a peculiar way into the opposing worlds of dice and people (Figure 3).

DREAM, PHANTASY, AND CHILDREN'S PLAY   81

Figure 3. Squiggle game with Mark: the world of dice and the world of people.

He explained to me that the dice were alive. They would jump up and then land, showing the number you had wished for. He drew entrances to the two worlds in the centre, and on the right, at the bottom, there was a button for the bell which he marked K (for *Klingel* = bell in German) so that one could get in. To me it seemed a striking image of his need to have somewhere to be. On the other hand his world of dice was also a magic world in which things happened that one could not foresee or expect—such as would normally only happen in a dream—but that was in fact the case in his life. So the world of dice seemed to me to represent a threatening world. And there were no living beings in it at all. He warded off this threat with magical, omnipotent manoeuvres: he only had to wish for something and it would happen. The dice leapt up and landed showing the number he wished for. But his real wish was to be allowed to have access to the world and to be able to decide himself where he would land; and be with people.

Instead of that, working on his own squiggle, he built up this threatening, bizarre world governed by magic powers. I had to draw exactly what he told me to. I, too, had to be completely under his magic control—which was a mirroring of the way the dice leapt and fell in our relationship. Everything was done as he wished it to be—so we had landed in a dream he was dreaming—and this was understandable as a use of magic that ensured he could escape from the danger lying hidden in relationships in his experience. I had to draw a crocodile with enormous teeth (Figure 4) and then an elephant with a trunk and tusks.

Figure 4. Squiggle game with Mark: a crocodile with enormous teeth.

He explained that these were fantasy animals, they were connected by their skins, the crocodile's teeth were the elephant's teeth and the tusks were the crocodile's teeth, and with its trunk the elephant could suck up dust, it was a cleaning machine. If a burglar came the crocodile could bite, and if he made a mess then the elephant would suck up the mess and it would be put inside the crocodile where it would be turned into earth. So his confused story centred around archaic things such as breaking in, being swallowed, incorporated, and so on. It was also about primitive, aggressive things that he elaborated here in his imagination and it was about controlling all this with magic power—since I had to draw things exactly as he wanted me to.

The next thing he drew from my squiggle was a fish with gigantic teeth (Figure 5).

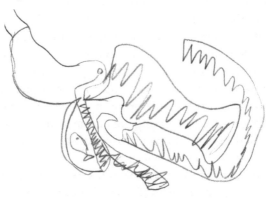

Figure 5. Squiggle with Mark: a fish with gigantic teeth.

This, he said, was a fantasy animal that was even more dangerous. All those were teeth. In the end he found a way out of this dangerous constellation. The small fish, he said, could sometimes survive because the big fish sometimes swallowed them whole. He did not like the little fish, he remarked (but they stayed whole), whereas he chopped up the shark. The story began to get out of control; the shark swallowed the fish and he (the fantasy animal) gobbled up the shark and chopped it into small pieces so that he could have lots of meat. And at its hind end (with the tail, on the right) the fantasy animal could bite and scratch itself. Finally it was a wild thicket, everything was scribbled over with aggressive, destructive fantasies and even the victim, the shark, was armed with extremely destructive, dangerous-looking teeth and had become an attacker who swallowed little fishes. One could perhaps only survive by being very small. Making himself invisible was possibly his predominant defence mechanism. What was remarkable was that on the other hand, from the experience of neglect, he had developed a kind of out-of-control greediness in eating so that it was probable that the destructive greed he depicted was also a part of his experience of how he was and of his unconscious fantasies about himself: unconsciously he experienced himself as someone who had destroyed his mother; as mentioned earlier she was a chronic drug addict.

In the next picture Mark extended this destructive world with a death's head (Figure 6).

Figure 6. Squiggle game with Mark: a death's head and a brain.

He explained that the death's head in the centre of the page was holding on to the person so that he didn't fall down. But it also dragged the person down and then he was dead. That was the spot on the right under the death's head. There was something next to it but he said he was not going to tell me what it was. I was to guess what it was. He literally shivered in revulsion. He gave me a hint that it was something that we use to think with; it was therefore the brain. One could surely say here that he was formulating, or rather drawing, the fact that thinking functions too were being destroyed. Possibly his revulsion at the picture alluded to what he had felt when his mother was under the influence of drugs, and he had linked this experience with the destruction of the ability to think. The otter had eaten the meat and just left the skin, he told me. The blue dot above the death's head with the line next to it was the brain and the figure next to that was the skin. He carried his destructiveness to the point of making the body fall apart. Initially Mark laughed and giggled quite a bit as he drew the picture as if preparing for the chilling scene. So I spoke to him about his fear. His reply was that he liked *nightmares* but if this really happened he would be scared. The initial manic defence gradually made way for a serious involvement with his fear.

Before the next picture I announced that each of us could now draw just one more picture. With great enjoyment he made it really difficult for me by producing a completely chaotic squiggle (Figure 7).

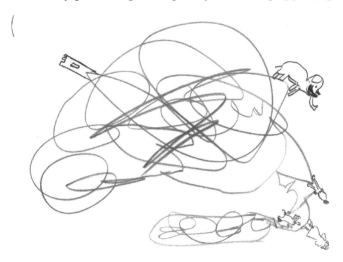

Figure 7. Squiggle game with Mark: castle, elephant, otter and crocodile.

He laughed when he had finished and said "finished". Then he told me once again what I had to draw and I obediently did what he said. First of all he wanted me to draw a castle, or an elephant, or a feline predator, or an otter, or a crocodile. The castle, he said, was standing on a thorn. The elephant also had to stand on a thorn and the person, too, was standing *right* on a thorn. They were all injured—only Ute (the carer at the children's home) was not standing on a spine. The dog, too, was stung twice. They all had to go to Ute—no, they all had to go to the castle, he said. He had got everything together again, the elephant from the previous story, and the danger and the destructiveness, but now all this was opposite the castle I had drawn, an element that he took up again. Ute was also there, whom he clearly experienced as strong and reassuring. He brought the two sides into connection with one another so that I assumed that he had understood something about his inner world and about needing to bring things together.

Finally, he drew a Shopping-kangaroo-robot (Figure 8) which jumped all over the shop and you could put things in the front of it.

And at the front on its head it had a few arrows in case anyone attacked it. The arrows on the front of its snout were then coloured in. "The person" operated the "Shopping-kangaroo-robot", Mark explained, and he added the person. I asked if this was Mark but no, it was Ute, someone you had to take along with you to go shopping. Once again he had created a quirky object out of a combination of elements—which is something that one finds in the dreams of adults

Figure 8. Squiggle game with Mark: "Shopping-kangaroo-robot" and Ute.

or in psychotic illnesses. This object had a lot to do with Ute and her function of caring for him on the one hand, but on the other hand it had something of the robot-like character of his mother when she was under the influence of drugs. A third point was that this object was at first exposed without protection to threatening attacks and then became threatening itself. With this last picture I again felt the description of his strange inner object world with its markedly bizarre features was very little controlled by secondary process re-working.

A year and half later I met Mark again, and this time it was the final examination before he left the home and returned to his foster family. He made a balloon out of my first squiggle and set to straightaway to colour it in, perhaps a little too positively and exuberantly. Out of my second squiggle he made a bean and an alien (Figure 9).

The alien was planting the bean, he told me. When he had more he was going to make bean soup out of them. I was impressed at how humorously he came out with this, how unthreatening the alien seemed in comparison with the pictures in our first interview, and how well he was able to feed himself. And it gave me a feeling of hope that Mark was going to be able to take something away with him from his stay at the Therapeutic Care Home. Again this picture and the narrative that accompanied it are hard to distinguish from an account of a dream. Among the other pictures he drew this time there was a tree planted firmly with a clear outline. So that altogether this presented a picture of a strikingly changed, now apparently very stable identity development on a completely different level in psychical terms.

Figure 9. Squiggle game with Mark: alien with bean.

A crocodile's tail and the little gate to heaven

Kevin was four years and eight months old when I saw him. He grew up with his mother who said of herself that the smallest frustration made her hit the ceiling. A grown-up half-brother also lived in the family, and so had Kevin's so-called grandfather until his violent death. This grandfather was described as being brutal in the extreme. He had, for instance, in a fit of rage, killed the family dog with an axe. He had originally been the father-in-law but then was later the mother's partner. Mother and brother together beheaded the grandfather when Kevin was three and a half years old, and the child was then placed in a children's home. Kevin was described as restless, and though noisy and rough with other children, also timid. He was hardly able to play. The slightest frustrations produced acts of instant, wild aggression after which he ran off.

In the interview with me he kept smiling at me, unsure of what to expect. I suggested we should play the squiggle game. In his first picture (Figure 10) he drew something underneath my squiggle which he told me in a whisper was a "tail".

He said it was a crododile's tail. Then a "nose" was added, and then two "tyres", so it was a car. At this point he nearly burst himself laughing, like the imp Rumpelstiltskin. Then this object became a ship and in the end a "plane". "It's flying up into the sky, it's flying up to

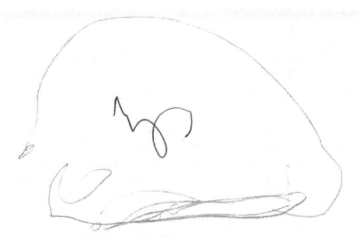

Figure 10. Squiggle game with Kevin: crocodile's tail, nose, car.

Figure.11. Squiggle game with Kevin: Little Gate to Heaven.

the Little Gate to Heaven." In my drawing I picked up this idea of the Gate to Heaven (Figure 11) and he added "hair" to the gate.

His next two drawings were of snakes "crawling". One of them turned into a tortoise. When we were talking about it, and I commented that a tortoise could draw itself back into its shell, his response was, this one cannot get away. This tortoise had spoken. It had bitten the snake open. There was a wardrobe with all the clothes in it and the tortoise had smashed it. Finally the last squiggle was turned into a flying bird. No, it was a balloon. When I said one could prick it and it would burst he fell on it saying "I want to go prick!" and he pricked it repeatedly and wildly with his pencil making holes in the paper. Finally he showed me where he had cuts on several of his fingers and described to me with great insistence how something had been cut off his finger and a lot of blood had poured out. They had flown to the doctor in a helicopter. He repeated his description of this scene several times.

It is immediately clear that Kevin was full of fears but equally full of aggressive fantasies. The mingling of the two elements of fear and destructiveness meant they were incomprehensible to him, so much so that he lost control of his ability to think. Aggression (crocodile's tail), fleeing (tyres, ship, plane), rescue (the Gate to Heaven—perhaps the grandfather is in Heaven?) were wildly jumbled as in a hectic dream, with his inner states flashing faster and faster past him: the tortoise bites the snake, smashes the wardrobe, the bird flies, here comes a balloon, a helicopter, the doctor! The most tangible thing that remains is the fear that something has been cut off—though he had certainly not been told this with reference to his grandfather's head—but that dominated his imagination.

Two things seemed to me to be of clinical importance: the fixation on fear and aggression that he could no longer get out of his mind, and the destruction of any ordered form of thinking that would first be required to enable any processing of violent feelings. With the ability to think in an ordered fashion so destroyed, Kevin was left unprotected and exposed to the feeling of helplessness and confusion. He understood neither himself nor the world around him. And despite this he tried in this conversation with me to start to build some shaky sense of order into his thinking with the help of a narrative that came across as a dream he might have had: something had been cut off his finger, it had bled a lot and they had been flown in a helicopter to the doctor. He certainly knew that I was a doctor.

Final comments and summary

1. In children's analyses dreams are rather rarely recounted. They are often simple in structure and their central message is relatively easy to decipher.
2. Dreams undergo a developmental process, as do all psychical activities. The development of dream-work and dream distortion in the stricter sense of the word does not appear until the child is around five years old or more. With the help of its dream-like thinking the child may identify with its mother's reverie and thereby with her α-function and may thus internalise the α-function.
3. The dreams of adults show many similarities to children's thinking. Or, to put it the other way round, children's thinking when awake, particularly in their play and in their imagination, as it appears in fantasies, is very much closer to adult dream thinking than it is to adult conscious thinking. It is often not clear from children's narratives where the boundaries are between fantasy, play, and dream.
4. Dreams, play, and the imaginative activity of children are genuine problem-solving thought processes. Children try with

the aid of these to cope with their inner conflicts. They give visual form to their inner structures in this way. I term the processing of β-elements in visual forms of dreamlike thinking, which one could also call pictograms, the α1 function (Günter, 2010). And I regard this α1 function as a precondition for any language-based, conceptual processing of sense perceptions and affects in the sense of an α2 function.

Notes

1. cf. among others, Hortig and Moser (2012), Jiménez (2012), Varvin et al. (2012), Weinstein and Ellman (2012) in the special issue "Traum—Theorie und Deutung" in *Psyche*, 9–10, 2012.
2. Names and some biographical details have been changed for reasons of discretion.

References

Fonagy, P., Gergely, G., Jurist, E., & Target, M. (2002). *Affect Regulation, Mentalization and the Development of the Self*. New York: Other Press.
Freud, S. (1908e). Creative writers and daydreaming. S. E., 9: 141-154. London: Hogarth.
Freud, S. (1916-1917). *Introductory Lectures on Psycho-Analysis*. S. E., 15–16: 1–240, 241–463. London: Hogarth.
Freud, S. (1920g). *Beyond the Pleasure Principle*. S. E., 18: 1–64. London: Hogarth.
Freud, S. (1930a). *Civilization and its Discontents*. S. E., 21: 57–146. London: Hogarth.
Grotjahn, M. (1938). Dream observations in a two-year-four-months-old baby. *Psychoanalytic Quarterly*, 7: 507–513.
Günter, M. (2010). Das Squiggle-Spiel in der therapeutischen Arbeit—Dialog und problemlösendes Denken. In: G. Dammann & T. Meng (Eds.), *Spiegelprozesse in Psychotherapie und Kunsttherapie* (pp. 89–101). Göttingen: Vandenhoeck und Ruprecht.
Hortig, V., & Moser, U. (2012). Interferenzen neurotischer Prozesse und introjektiver Beziehungsmuster im Traum. *Psyche—Zeitschrift für Psychoanalyse und ihre Anwendungen*, 66: 889–916.
Jiménez, J. P. (2012). Tradition und Erneuerung in der Traumdeutung. *Psyche—Zeitschrift für Psychoanalyse und ihre Anwendungen*, 66: 803–832.

Koukkou, M., & Lehmann, D. (1980). Psychophysiologie des Träumens und der Neurosentherapie. Das Zustands-Wechsel-Modell, eine Synopsis. *Fortschritte der Neurologie, Psychiatrie und ihrer Grenzgebiete, 48*: 324–350.

Koukkou, M., & Lehmann, D. (1983). Dreaming: the functional state-shift hypothesis. A neurophysiological model. *British Journal of Psychiatry, 142*: 221–231.

Koukkou, M., & Lehmann, D. (2000). Traum und Hirnforschung. In: B. Boothe (Ed.), *Der Traum—hundert Jahre nach Freuds Traumdeutung* (pp. 227–249). Zürich: vdf.

Lempp, R. (1984). Psychische Entwicklung und Schizophrenie. In: R. Lempp (Ed.), *Psychische Entwicklung und Schizophrenie* (pp. 9–12). Bern: Einführung und Zusammenfassung.

Lempp, R. (1991). *Vom Verlust der Fähigkeit, sich selbst zu betrachten. Eine entwicklungspsychologische Erklärung der Schizophrenie und des Autismus.* Bern: Huber.

Niederland, W. G. (1957). The earliest dreams of a young child. *Psychoanalytic Study of the Child, 12*: 190–208.

Varvin, S., Jovic, V., Rosenbaum, B., Fischmann, T., & Hau, S. (2012). Traumatische Träume: Streben nach Beziehung. *Psyche—Zeitschrift für Psychoanalyse und ihre Anwendungen, 66*: 937–967.

Weinstein, L., & Ellman, S. J. (2012). Die Bedeutung der endogenen Stimulation für das Träumen und für die Entwicklung: ein Versuch der Integration und Neuformulierung. *Psyche—Zeitschrift für Psychoanalyse und ihre Anwendungen, 66*: 862–888.

Winnicott, D. W. (1968). Playing: its theoretical status in the clinical situation. *International Journal Psycho-Analysis, 49*: 591–599.

CHAPTER SIX

On reflection in dreams or "Do people get lost if they go up in a hot air balloon?"

Daniel Barth

Anja, a seven-year-old girl, dreamt that she was flying high into the sky in a hot air balloon with her mother. When I asked her what this dream made her think of, she asked me in alarm, "Do people get lost if they go up in a hot air balloon?" Anja is afraid she and her mother will disappear into space and never come back. The balloon will only go in one direction and she is afraid there is no return. And, in fact, in the three-year analysis with Anja things did only go in a single direction, and that was over-excitation, meaning that she did "get lost". For a long time she was rarely able to calm down.

In the clinical comments on Anja's dream, I propose to take up the "psychical apparatus" depicted in Chapter Seven of Freud's *Interpretation of Dreams* (1900a). He describes it as an apparatus of reflection, and Anja's dream has encouraged me to explore the concepts of *reflex*, *reflection-as-mirroring*, and *reflection-for-thinking*. Reflection-as-mirroring is important in that Freud assumed that the progressive stream of thoughts in a dream is transformed into a regressive one. I shall explore the question of whether reflection-as-mirroring develops in the psychical apparatus into a reflection-for-thinking. In the conclusion, I wish to describe how my thoughts on reflection have changed my clinical understanding and have enabled me to take new paths in interpretation.

Freud's linear model of the Psyche

Freud's model of the psyche is one of energy, founded on the concept of the instinctual drive. It is the task of the psychical apparatus to deal with psychical energy. One could object that this model is very rough and therefore represents an inadmissible simplification. But the model—with a few modifications—could in fact still be relevant: to use Bion's terms (1962) one could say that *content* (♂), that is, psychical energy, is taken into the *container* (♀), that is, a psychical apparatus, and processed there.

In this paper I shall show how Bion's reverie can very well be compared to what goes on in the psychical apparatus as Freud described it in 1900. Freud's concept of the pre-conscious has the role of the α-function that is connected to reflection-for-thinking. Before he developed the concept of the psychical apparatus of 1900, Freud had already designed two models, the first of which is found in his *Project for a Scientific Psychology* (1950a[1895]).

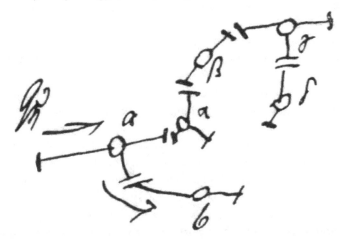

In this model he proposes an apparatus consisting of a sequence of neurons. The branching off from neuron α in the direction of the arrow towards neuron β represents the direct discharge of energy. If, however, a part of the psychical energy passes via neurons α, β, γ, and δ, then a lesser charge will pass through β. Freud saw this restraint or inhibition as the basic precondition for the existence of an ego. (Freud, 1950a[1895], p. 324). But only a year later, in a letter to Fliess in 1896, he dismissed this neuron model and sketched the following psychical apparatus:

```
         I              II              III
W         Wz            Ub              Vb            Bews
×  ×———×   ×———×   ×———×   ×———×   ×
×         ×   ×            ×               ×
              ×
```

In this model, Freud hypothesised various psychical structures that he depicted in a linear sequence. Here W = *Wahrnehmung* is perception, Wz = *Wahrnehmungszeichen* are the signs of perception (i.e., the first transcription of the perception), Ub = *Unbewusstheit*[1] is the unconsciousness (or second transcription), Vb = *Vorbewusstsein* the pre-conscious (the third transcription corresponding to the ego), and Bews = *Bewusstsein* is consciousness. The bracketed comments are as they appear in the Freud text.

Three years later, in the *Interpretation of Dreams* (1900a), Freud returned to this model. A perception (W) strikes the psychical apparatus, undergoes an unknown process and this leads to a motor reaction (M). The movement is one of discharge from left to right.

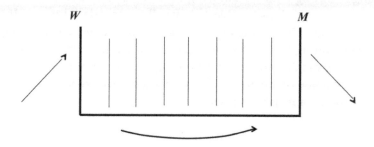

This model corresponds to a classic black box. We have an input (W = perception) and an output (M = motor activity). In between these two, a process takes place that is referred to as a black box because it is unknown. The black box model is well known in science to describe processes that we do not as yet understand. But in fact

Freud at the same time introduced some modes of functioning of the apparatus:

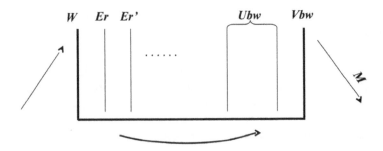

A stimulus reaching perception (*W*) triggers a memory trace (*Er* for *Erinnerung*) in the psychical apparatus that is followed by other, later memories (*Er'*, *Er"*, etc.).

It is not hard to recognise in this a further development of the signs of perception described in 1897. The memory traces meet the unconscious, and the resulting process is by definition (since it is unconscious) inaccessible to our consciousness. The functioning of the unconscious belongs to primary process admitting no contradiction and unbound by time. In the next step, the information reaches the pre-conscious in a form modified by the unconscious. The function of the pre-conscious is manifold. According to Freud, the pre-conscious functions here above all as a censor, holding back information or letting it through and so allowing its entry into consciousness (here *M*). The pre-conscious is subject above all to secondary process. If the pre-conscious allows unconscious elements to enter consciousness, one can assume that further modifications will have taken place—in some cases making the content unrecognisable. Before speaking of a further function of the pre-conscious I would now like to report on the first sessions of Anja's analysis.

The ghosts

When she began her analysis with me (coming for four sessions a week), Anja was six years old. In the course of this analysis, which lasted over three years, we repeatedly met with difficulties because Anja reacted to the slightest psychical tension with a great and almost uncontrollable agitation. She had lived in a children's home since she was four years old as her mother was a drug addict and bulimic. The mother, who died a year after the analysis was over, consumed so much alcohol that the only regular contact she had with Anja was when she, the mother, was hospitalised in a psychiatric unit.

At these times she swore that Anja was the most important thing in the world to her, that she loved her above everything in her life. This however did not prevent her from returning to drinking such massive quantities of alcohol when she was discharged that she did not, in fact, visit her daughter for months. Contact with Anja's father, who was also an addict, had been broken off. In the first session with me Anja drew a radiant sun: everything was fine, she had no fears even at night, she said, because she had an Indian dream catcher over her bed. In the second session she told me that she loved me so much and that she wanted to stay with me always. At the end of the third month it became clear how dangerous this was: on a cold November evening Anja and I were sitting on the balcony of my office. She had put a candle on the ground and lit it. I sat down on a low chair next to her. Without warning she jumped up on to my lap: it was so nice to be here with me, she said. While I was considering how to understand this sudden and exaggerated closeness to me, Anja explained there were ghosts out there in the dark and she was afraid of them. I wondered why she saw ghosts just at the moment when she had made herself "safe" on my lap. Her mother had always created an over-close relationship with her but had then turned her back on the child to follow her own need for drugs. When I gave an interpretation along these lines, "the ghosts can see us and don't want us to be so nice and snug here", Anja became extremely agitated and tried to hide behind or almost inside me, she was so terrified of the ghosts. Her agitation barely subsided, and I did not feel that closeness to me was helpful to her, quite the contrary. So I wondered what my remark had triggered. It will certainly have reactivated earlier experiences of relationships being broken off (her mother's bulimic relationship pattern), and also Anja may have felt that my interpretation "they don't want us to be so *nice and snug* here" was dangerously seductive. This episode taught me how little it took for Anja to be completely overwhelmed by her feelings. Looking at this in terms of Freud's dream model one could say that Anja's pre-conscious (*Pcs.*) was in danger of drowning in the flood of stimuli from both conscious (*Cs.*) and unconscious (*Ucs.*), and that this was why she reacted with almost uncontrollable motor hyperactivity. My remark had not helped to reassure her but had increased her agitation for some reason. Anja was mentally and emotionally too fragile to take in my interpretation. With hindsight, it might have been better to have said "there are ghosts out there watching us and listening to the two of us talking about ghosts". A more neutral triangulation of this kind would have given Anja more psychical space.

Freud (1900a), Chapter 7a

Freud initially saw the psychical apparatus as a reflex system. "The old basic conceptual schema of neurology", as Karl Jaspers put it in 1973:

> is the idea of the organism being subjected to stimuli to which it reacts after inner processing (process of excitation) with movements or other objectively perceptible manifestations. One has to imagine this physiological process of excitation as being of extreme complexity. It is conceived of as tiers of reflexes upon reflexes in a system of interlocking functions. (p. 130)

The function of a reflex apparatus is to trigger a reaction to a piece of information in as precise and unique a form as possible. Thus a reflex is an involuntary, rapid, and uniform reaction of an organism to a particular stimulus. A typical simple reflex is the patellar tendon reflex, which is triggered by a light blow to the tendon just under the knee-cap. As a reflex response it produces a contraction of the quadriceps muscle and knee extension. This simple reflex is produced by an impulse to the spinal cord and without the involvement of the brain. But it is only limited in its functioning—it does not enable the control of complex movements as, for example, walking or running. For walking or running to be possible, the automatic reflex has to be partially inhibited—and as such influenced—by the higher centres of the brain. The simple reflex is not cancelled out but is put under the control of a higher centre in the brain, which in turn can function on the basis of reflexes.

Freud, however, in contrast to Vladimir Blechterev and Ivan Petrovitsch Pavlov, was not impressed by the chain-reflex theory. In this theory it is assumed that the result of one reflex triggers the next reflex and so on. Freud was not interested in reflecting on reflex actions but rather on the functioning of reflected actions. I should now like to take a closer look at the three concepts of reflex, reflection-as-mirroring, and reflection-for-thinking.[2]

All three go back to the Latin verb *reflectere*, meaning turning back or bending. The question is how these three terms are connected. Reflex and reflection-as-mirroring are similar mechanisms: a stimulus meets an apparatus such as a mirror and is "thrown back" by it. A predefined modification of the stimulus occurs in the apparatus or mirror—and it is returned in changed or mirrored form. Examples here are the patellar reflex mentioned above and the mirror image. Advocates of the reflex chain theory hold the view that the cause of every state is derived from its previous states. The apparatus reacts to the environment in such a differentiated manner that it can be assumed to have enough differentiated and complex reflexes available to it. So, according to this theory, all states can be explained: instinctual drive discharge can be understood as a simple reflex function, and an external or internal stimulus will produce a predictable reaction.

But what is the picture in the case of reflection-for-thinking? Freud was convinced that since we have to deal with complex reality, we need a means of modifying the discharge of instinctual drive.

> The exigencies of life interfere with this simple function [i.e., instinctual drive discharge via reflex function] and it is to them [i.e., the exigencies of life] too that the apparatus owes the impetus to further development. (Freud, 1900a, p. 565, my intervention)

Undoubtedly, the ability to reflect in the sense of reflection-for-thinking is one of the greatest achievements of the psychical apparatus. But does reflection-for-thinking build upon reflection-as-mirroring? Or do they have nothing in common? It is in the nature of dreaming that the perception of the external world and motility are both greatly reduced.

Two elements are central in the Freudian model of the dream: the first is the delay of gratification of needs, the second, regression. Regression describes what is happening when "the excitation moves in a *backward* direction" (Strachey's italics rendering Freud's double-spacing of the word, p. 542).

Instead of being transmitted towards the *motor* end of the apparatus it moves towards the sensory end and finally reaches the perceptual system. If we describe as "progressive" the direction taken by psychical processes arising from the unconscious during waking life, then we may speak of dreams as having a "regressive" character. (p. 542)

Freud speaks of an "alteration in the normal psychical procedure which makes possible the cathexis of the system *Pcpt*. in the reverse direction, starting from thoughts, to the pitch of complete sensory vividness" (p. 543). I return now to Freud's schema of the psyche of 1900. In this concept the current flows from (*Pcpt*) perception to (*Ucs*) unconscious, is filtered by the (*Pcs*) pre-conscious, and finally flows into motility.

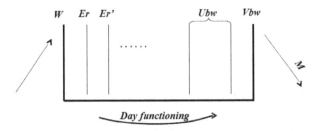

In dreaming, as in thinking, an added backward flow occurs alongside the usual forward flow. Instead of unconscious thoughts being simply transported automatically or filtered in a forward direction, they undergo a re-flection and are carried in a regressive flow, returning to the psychical apparatus. But in dreams there are also forward moving processes at work because of the gradient from perception to motor activity, and in this way a feedback loop develops that contains both forward and backward flows. This is possible by virtue of reflection-as-mirroring.

The memory traces, which have been triggered by perceptions and have then passed through the unconscious, are reflected. This means they have to pass through the unconscious again thus taking a retrogressive course. They are mirrored back and create fresh memory traces (*Er'*, *Er"* . . .). If these traces do not reach perception they are carried with the forward flow of the model back to the right and there, passing through the unconscious, to the pre-conscious again. If, however, the memory traces either reach perception (*W*) or enter (*M*) motility, the dreamer wakes up.

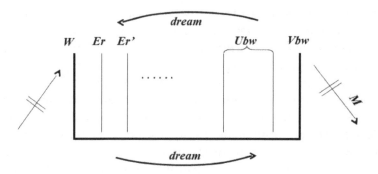

In dreaming the back and forth movement of the memory traces is a continuous process in the course of which they are continuously modified. Thus one can regard dreaming as a process leading to a continuous alteration of the dream content through multiple mirrorings. In 1911 Freud not only postulated "that thinking was originally unconscious" (1911b, p. 221), but rather "Thinking was endowed with characteristics which made it possible for the mental apparatus to tolerate an increase of stimulus while the process of discharge was postponed. It is essentially an experimental kind of acting" (p. 221).

If we follow Ogden's reading of Freud and Bion, then dreaming, reverie, is the precondition for thinking. What could trial action have meant in the dream model of 1900? The dream thought meeting the pre-conscious could be channelled into motor activity—but then the dream would be broken off. The thought, however, can be taken as a trial thought and be mirrored back, taking on a retrogressive character. It is then altered as it passes through the unconscious, is caught again in the progressive current, and runs through the unconscious another time before again meeting the pre-conscious. This back and forth movement is similar to a simulation: in a simulation experiments are carried out in a model set-up to gain insights into the actual system.

Experiments with rats in a labyrinth (Louie & Wilson, 2000) have shown that a partial function of the night-time brain activity does in fact seem to be a form of simulation. Electrodes were implanted into the rats' brains. In the case of half of the rats it could be shown that while (in their) sleep they were repeating the brain patterns they had shown while they were running through the labyrinth in the day-time. The rats in this half of the sample, whose EEG pattern in the night was a repetition of their daytime labyrinth running pattern, found their way through better the next day than the rats in the other half. It can therefore be assumed that the rats who repeated the brain patterns of the day in their sleep were not merely dreaming but that with this brain pattern, which occurred just as in humans mainly in the rapid eye movement (REM) phase, they were able to use the night-time brain activity as "training" for the next day. Dreaming can thus be regarded as mental action in a trial form. Trial actions are carried out and these—just as in a simulation—are continuously altered in a feed-back mechanism. Reflection-for-thinking presupposes reflection-as-mirroring in dreaming—for without mirroring no regressive stream of thoughts can occur. But this does not answer the question of how the simple reflection-as-mirroring develops into complex reflection-for-thinking.

Let me now turn again to a dream that Anja had and to the question of reflection in clinical work. After that I wish go further into the question of where reflection might take place—under the aegis of which intra-psychical instance.

The dream

It was after four months of analysis, one month after the incident of the ghosts on the balcony, that Anja told me of the short dream I recounted at the beginning of this paper. "I dreamt of flying up high in the sky in a hot air balloon with Mummy." Anja drew a picture of the dream; her mother is holding her spectacles in her hand. I asked her what the dream made her think of and she asked "Do people get lost up there? How do they get back down to earth?" Her fear was very clear that she would disappear with her mother, whom she missed so much: there would be no way back. In the interpretation I then offered, I took up her fear of losing herself with or in her mother and introduced a third person. "Barth," I said, referring to myself, "is down here watching Anja and her mother flying up into the sky in the hot air balloon." Anja became pensive and was quite quiet for a moment. This quietness was possibly the result of my interpretation: I had taken up her fear and offered a triangulation.

But very soon afterwards, Anja's excited state returned and she went on drawing. "This figure here is Barth and Anja is shouting out of the balloon basket 'Gagi Bart' " ("Shit Barth" in Swiss German). She and her mother are laughing at Barth who is so stupid and a cripple too. And as if that is not enough they are throwing shit down on to him. What has happened?

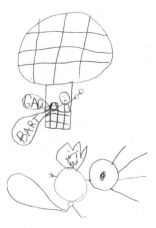

Anja had at first been relieved that I understood her fear and had introduced myself into the picture as a third person. For a brief moment her fear of disappearing into the sky was contained, her balloon was given a tether on the ground. The agitation that followed can certainly be understood as a manic defence against depressive anxieties. The triangulation is warded off because leaving the dyad forever appears to be too painful.

But I should like to return to Anja's association to the dream when she asked: "Do people get lost up there?" It is the urgent question here whether we—she and I—together will have developed the ability not only to fly up there but also to return safely.

Can I bind her agitation with my analytic function and mirror it back to her in a modified form? Anja's fear that she will not return from the trip with her mother—or her analyst—is explicit. Formulated in a different analytic terminology it is the question of whether the beta elements now re-experienced in the relationship can, as Ferro (2005, p. 1540) wittily put it, be "alphabetized" through the alpha function, or whether the overflowing content ($\male$) will find a sufficiently large container ($\female$). The first four months helped Anja to dream. She is now daring to enter into a new kind of relationship. Dreaming has become possible because for a while she can tolerate her fear and so hold back her motor restlessness. Together we can now—at least for a while—do some thinking: Anja can tell me of her fear of getting lost up in the sky with her mother and I can reflect on this fear with her. But this ability still quickly breaks down in the analysis.

Freud (1900a), Chapter 7b

Reflection-as-mirroring is the precondition for the regression, the backward flow, needed for dreaming to take place. Freud saw two reasons for the backward flow of the stream of thoughts:

> We have put forward the view that in all probability this regression, wherever it may occur, is an effect of a resistance opposing the progress of a thought into consciousness along the normal path and of a simultaneous attraction exercised upon the thought by the presence of memories possessing great sensory force. (p. 547)

Thus, regression is centrally linked with resistance and repression. Whereas reflection-as-mirroring can take place without the presence of an inner conflict, repression by definition presupposes such a conflict. Since, however, the human psyche begins to function before any repression takes place, Freud was forced to postulate primal repression in order to rescue his model. This primal repression led, he claimed, to a thought being pulled by the unconscious. It would undoubtedly be interesting to pursue this concept further but it seems to me a questionable procedure to "prove the validity" of the fundamental assumption that regression can only come about through a psychic conflict with the further fundamental assumption of primal repression. If our starting point is the mechanism of reflection then the preconscious in Freud's model of 1900 is the only instance where this refection can take place.

In the model of 1900 the only intra-psychical instance available to receive and create the reflection of memory traces is the pre-conscious. The pre-conscious acts as a selective, interactive mirror that, alongside the two functions described by Freud, in my view performs a third:

1. the pre-conscious allows some psychical energy to pass through (Freud)
2. the pre-conscious binds some energy (Freud)
3. the pre-conscious reflects psychical energy (acting as a mirror).

Dreaming only becomes possible if there is a reflective instance in the psychical apparatus that throws back the unconscious content, thus making it once again available to the psychical apparatus.

After passing through the unconscious, the memory traces, now re-triggered, will return to the pre-conscious in newly altered form. Here at the mirror of the pre-conscious they enter consciousness, or are bound, or are once again reflected.

This back and forth movement allows psychical progression and regression and is the enabler of dreaming and thinking processes. One can visualise the pre-conscious as a half-permeable mirror of some kind of glass allowing psychical energy to flow through unimpeded (function 1). It binds psychical energy (function 2) and in this process condensation appears on the glass. This layer enables the forming of a reflection as in a mirror (function 3). Before I pursue the question of how the pre-conscious is formed I should like to return to the analysis with Anja. With the work of analysis it had become possible for her to cathect me as a helpful object, and as a result she was faced with how to deal with my absence over the holidays.

The postcard

After a year and half of analysis I received a postcard from her, sent from where she was on holiday, with the following drawing on the back.

When the sessions started again Anja commented on it and said she had had such a wonderful time with her mother—I knew in fact that she had been away without her mother! I remarked that Anja was wearing spectacles in the picture (she does not in fact need to wear spectacles). She explained that she was wearing the spectacles because she was the mother. She was now Mummy–Anja. The idea of separation is pushed away as if to say "I am the mother so there is no separation". I did not take this up directly but commented that Barth did not look happy i n the picture. Her response was "Barth is afraid". Knowing how precarious Anja's balance was I did not wish to endanger the newly achieved triangulation. Anja would not have been able to digest either an interpretation of the manic defence on the one hand, or the projection of her fear into me on the other. She had been able to survive in the holidays and had been allowed to be in "seventh heaven" with her mother through projecting the elements that frightened her into me, and yet she also knew that the analyst was a guarantee that she would not get lost in her identification with her mother. I confined myself therefore to an analyst-centred interpretation (Steiner, 1994) that I extended with the knowledge of our being "three": "Barth was alone on holiday so perhaps he didn't have a good time but he saw that Anja and her mother were together and now Anja is here again." This was reassuring for Anja and made it easier for her to start again in the analysis. In conclusion I should like to elaborate some thoughts on the development of the pre-conscious.

The pre-conscious and the α-function

Freud was dissatisfied right from the beginning with the purely intrapsychical model of thinking as he could not quite understand the beginnings of pre-consciousness. Freud tried to defend his intrapsychical model of dream formation by presupposing a primal repression (1915e, p. 180). Primal repression remains, however, an awkward concept of a distinctly hypothetical nature. This was one reason why he repeatedly, if rather unsystematically, turned to the early mother–child relationship, writing of the "experienced person" (1950a[1895], p. 318), the "extraneous help" (1900a, p. 565), or of "repeated situations of satisfaction" (1926d, p. 170). In 1900 he stated that if the hungry child is left alone its state of need will remain the same. "A change can only come about if in some way or other (in the case of the baby, through outside help) an 'experience of satisfaction' can be achieved which puts an end to the internal stimulus" (1900a, p. 565).

The baby is thus in a situation of "biological helplessness" (1926d, p. 139) that it cannot overcome by its own means. In one radical statement Freud maintains that the psychical apparatus cannot develop without the co-operation of a second person. It is only in the relationship to the mother (the primary object) that the psychical apparatus can develop. The primary object takes over three functions that could also be ascribed to the pre-conscious:

1. The mother satisfies the baby's primary needs.
2. She binds parts of psychical energy (β-elements, content ♂) by means of projective identification. The affects are taken in by the mother and in this way the baby can postpone the satisfaction of its needs with reassuring and calming effect.
3. She mirrors the psychical processes of the baby. In doing this the mother is far from passive, she is actively participating in the baby's affects (function 2), she processes these in reverie, or in other words in the α-function, and mirrors (function 3) the psychical state of the baby in modulated form (Fonagy et al., 2002, p. 93).

These three functions, satisfying needs, binding psychical energy, and mirroring enable the baby to develop its psychical apparatus within the relationship with its primary object. All three processes are complex and reappear in the functions of the pre-conscious.

This now leads me to my clinical conclusions: as I have shown in the case of Anja it is important that interpretations are made on these three levels. At first in the analysis with Anja it most often made no sense to make her conscious of her inner conflicts. I learnt to offer partial satisfaction for her agitated affects (function 1) and to bind them in a painful process of projective identification (function 2) in order to create a mirroring surface. In this way, but only at a later stage, mirroring in the sense of function 3 became possible.

The following two years of analysis with Anja made heavy demands on me as they were far from straightforward or easy. One of the greatest problems, as mentioned above, was the way Anja so quickly became agitated. It took me a long time to understand that as the analyst I was contributing to this agitation and even fanning the flames by trying too hard to understand what was going on in the transference and countertransference. In the terms of the dream model described above one could say that I did not succeed in keeping the quantity of memory traces ($\male$ = content) small enough to prevent the agitation in her psychical apparatus ($\female$ = container) from becoming too extreme and spilling over into the conscious by perception (*W*) or movement (*M*). Because the analytical pair kept "waking up" prematurely the back and forth movement necessary for thinking was interrupted far too soon, and this made progress impossible.

Over time I succeeded in maintaining the "sleep" needed for reverie in the analysis so that the process of reflection-for-thinking was able to grow in Anja and in myself.

Notes

1. Freud only used the term *Unbewusstheit* (unconsciousness) twice in his works: 1896 in this letter to Fliess, and in 1910 in *Contributions to the Psychology of Love*. (He replaced the word unconsciousness with unconscious in the editions after 1925.)
2. The term reflection-for-thinking is used to mean a form of reflection leading to thinking. The terms "thinking" and "reflection" are not to be regarded as identical here. Freud assumes that a retrogressive flow of the stream of thoughts is necessary for thinking to develop. None of these three terms is to be equated with the philosophical sense of reflection referring to thinking about thinking. It is not reflection as meta-thought that is to be the subject of this paper but rather thoughts on what the beginnings of thinking might look like.

References

Bion, W. R. (1962). *Learning from Experience*. Heinemann: London.
Ferro, A. (2005). Bion: theoretical and clinical observations. *International Journal of Psycho-Analysis*, 86(6): 1535–1542.
Fonagy, P., Gergely, G., Jurist, E., & Target, M. (2002). *Affect Regulation, Mentalization and the Development of the Self*. New York: Other Press.
Freud, S. (1900a). *The Interpretation of Dreams. S. E.*, 4–5. London: Hogarth.

Freud, S. (1911b). Formulations on the two principles of mental functioning. *S. E., 12*: 213–226. London: Hogarth.
Freud, S. (1915e). The unconscious. *S. E., 14*: 159–215. London: Hogarth.
Freud, S. (1926d). *Inhibitions, Symptoms and Anxiety. S. E., 20*: 75–176. London: Hogarth.
Freud, S. (1950a[1895]). *Project for a Scientific Psychology. S. E., 1*: 281–391. London: Hogarth.
Jaspers, K. (1973). *Allgemeine Psychopathologie*. Berlin: Springerverlag (9. Auflage).
Louie, K., & Wilson, M. A. (2000). Temporally structured replay of awake hippocampal ensemble activity during rapid eye movement sleep. *Neuron, 29*: 145–156.
Steiner, J. (1994). Patient-centred and analyst-centered interpretations: some implications of containment and countertransference. *Psychoanalytic Inquiry, 14*: 406–422.

CHAPTER SEVEN

Dreams and narratives in the developmental process: Dreaming as perceived in developmental psychology and neurobiology

Kai von Klitzing

There is surprisingly little research on the significance of dreaming in the fields of developmental psychology and neurobiology. There are a number of reasons for this in terms of method. Dreaming is a profoundly subjective phenomenon and as such offers considerable barriers to established empirical research with its possible over-insistence on objectivity. In the study of dreaming, observable data has to be derived from the retrospective account of the subject, the dreamer. There is no way of checking the truth of the verbal descriptions of dreams: indeed the accounts of dreams are no more than indirect witnesses of the dream itself.

The discovery by Aserinsky and Kleitman (1953) of rapid eye movement (REM) sleep as a possible neuronal correlate of dreaming has therefore provided new input for research in developmental neuroscience. Hobson (2009) puts forward the hypothesis that REM sleep is "a protoconscious state providing, as it were, a virtual reality model of the world that is of functional use to the development and maintenance of waking consciousness" (p. 803).

That REM sleep is not the sole precondition for dreaming is apparent from the fact that REM sleep is already prevalent early in development, that is, during prenatal life and particularly in infancy.

By contrast, lucid dreaming does not occur in connection with REM sleep until the development of the brain has progressed far enough for the narrative organisation of subjective experience to be possible. In general, it is assumed that dreams resembling those of adults begin to occur between the ages of five and eight. Hobson (2009) assumes that REM sleep plays an important role in the development of the brain, even before dream consciousness appears. The researchers in Hobson's research group are ambivalent about the subjective meaning of dreams. For example, Hobson says he assumes that "dreaming is an indispensable—if sometimes misleading—subjective informant on what the brain does during REM sleep". As a consequence he states: "we may be bound to admit that dreaming itself could be an epiphenomenon without any direct effect on normal or abnormal cognition" (p. 805).

According to this view, REM sleep is protoconscious because it provides a virtual model of the world with imaginary agents/actors (the protoself) moving through a fictitious space and experiencing strong emotions. So REM sleep is a state that emerges before consciousness. A secondary consciousness then builds on the first. Establishing this demands that activity in cortical structures be appropriately modulated as we wake up or notice while dreaming that we *are* dreaming (Hobson, 2009, p. 808). Thus, according to this theory, REM sleep is a kind of neurobiological activity of the brain that prepares for the later development of consciousness. The subjective dream, that emerges in the course of the development of REM sleep, is seen as a kind of epiphenomenon of this state of protoconsciousness.

A connection between dreaming and early child development is also described by the Zurich researchers Lehmann and Koukkou who developed the "brain-physiological state-shift model of dreaming" (Koukkou & Lehmann, 2000).

> Brain states shift in the course of sleep phases. The formal features of the dreams that are remembered, such as associative visual vividness, the coherence of the episodic structure, the fragmentation of the storyline, the infantilisation of the dream self and of the other actors correspond in this model to the activation of memory representations at a low level of complexity. These visual memories at a low level of complexity stem from the early years of a child's development and can only be recalled in sleep—not in the waking state. The physiological regression of functional brain states leads to a situation in which

the process of dream creation and dream development uses "cognitive–emotional strategies of childhood". (p. 244)

Thus the authors conjecture that a physiological regression to simpler functional states takes place in sleep and that these are similar to earlier developmental states. In the process of this regression memory stores are opened, containing early memories and strategies of thinking. Thus states arise in which early memories and the cognitive strategies of the child are linked with later experiences of adulthood, and the memory levels of childhood become accessible again.

This would mean that dreaming resembles childlike thinking and narrative processes, so that in younger children the dream as it is recounted is likely to be closer to their waking thought structures than would be the case in adults. Is this why it is hard to draw a line between children's dreams and their stories, daydreams, games, and fantasies? Is this why the younger a child is, the less the form of the dream differs from other thought processes?

In contrast to Hobson's work, the theories of Kaplan-Solms (2000) are grounded in the tradition of neuro-psychoanalysis (cf. also Solms & Lechevalier, 2002). These authors carried out research into the neurostructural foundations of dreaming based on the examination of patients who had suffered certain brain lesions.

According to the authors, the following forms of brain damage may impair the ability to dream:

- Left inferior parietal-lobe lesions lead to loss of dreaming and loss of the ability to "extract higher-order abstractions from perceptual information in all modalities". The patients were not able to symbolise the information taken in (p. 48).
- Right inferior parietal-lobe lesions, alongside loss of dreaming, also lead to the loss of the ability "to concretely represent information mentally in a visuospatial medium".
- Frontal brain region lesions, alongside loss of dreaming, lead to adynamia and loss of spontaneous motivation (p. 50).
- Damage in the ventromesial occipital and temporal region leads to the loss of the ability to visualise both in dreaming and waking state (p. 51).
- Damage in the frontal limbic region leads to the loss of the ability to distinguish between dreams and real experiences and so to

a removal of "a factor that normally inhibits dreaming and dreamlike thinking (i.e., inhibits regression)" (p. 52) .
- Damage to the temporal limbic region leads to recurring stereotyped nightmares. Typical nightmarish auras also occur in temporal lobe epilepsies. The factor of affective arousal is ascribed to this region (p. 53).

So "the process of dreaming unfolds over a functional system composed of six fundamental component parts". But no particular function contributing to the ability to dream can be localised in any one of these regions. On the contrary the dynamic process unfolds as an interaction of the different component parts of the total functional system (p. 54). Thus Kaplan-Solms and Solms emphasise the network-like nature of the variously localised brain functions as forming the basis of dreaming.

The starting point of dreaming can be any stimulation of the brain during sleep. The activation of the motivational system necessary for dreaming is a response to the stimulus that first arouses the sleeping brain (e.g., the REM activation). Dreaming only occurs if a stimulus during sleep arouses motivational interest. These motivational programmes cannot discharge into motor activity because the person is asleep. "For this reason . . . the motivational programme appears to end in a perceptual rather than a motor act . . . The response to the arousing stimulus is represented symbolically in a spatial medium" (p. 55). The process ends in a concrete perceptual representation that is translated by the reflective systems as if it were a real experience.

"The dreaming process is initiated by a paradoxical conjunction of the state of sleep with relative forebrain activation" (Solms, 2011, p. 540). It takes place in the particular circumstance of a cortical deactivation through the state of sleep. The most frequent source of the forebrain activation is REM sleep activity. In contrast to Hobson's view, Solms' understanding is that REM activation, that is the mesopontine, is certainly not the sole source of forebrain activation to cause dreaming. On the contrary, even an intrinsic forebrain activity can be the trigger.

The paradoxical conjunction of sleep and activation is a necessary, but not sufficient, precondition for dreaming to happen. Specific front brain lesions result in the cessation of dreaming, although REM activity may still occur. Solms assumes that there is an additional specific variable that causes dreaming, and suggests the activation of certain limbic forebrain structures. Even if the way these are connected is not quite clear, it seems that networks with motivational drive and the surfacing of emotion are crucially involved.

There is a reversal here of the process of conscious perception. "The activation of the posterior cortical structures with perceptual (especially visual) imagery and memory" (Solms, 2011, p. 540) is the result and not the starting point of the activation process. According to Solms, dreaming is "1) a state of consciousness characterised by 2) reduced constraints and controls on 3) memory and perceptual imagery with 4) motivational incentive and emotional salience".

These neurobiological findings, however, still leave the significance of dreaming in psychological development unclear. Clearly the underlying brain–physiological processes must be important preconditions for healthy development. Specifically, however, dreams that can be recounted by the dreamer can only appear after the neurobiological and developmental function systems of symbolisation and narrative ability have matured. We know little about the significance of dreaming in children of pre-school and primary school age. If dreaming represents a regression to early processes of thinking and remembering, then young children are necessarily close to this stage of development and therefore their modes of thinking in dreaming and in reality are not very far removed from one another.

With regard to adolescence, the results of a study by the Basel research group centred around Brand, Hatzinger, and Holzbor-Trachsler are of interest (Brand et al., 2011).They carried out a survey of 5,580 adolescents looking at their sleep patterns, their recalling of dreams, and their mental–emotional development. The most important findings were that the ability to remember dreams was correlated with gender, creativity, and quality of sleep. Furthermore, the dreams seem to have influenced the person's mood on the following day. The researchers showed that female adolescents more frequently remembered their dreams and felt them to have a greater influence on their mood the following day than the same-age male adolescents. The frequency with which dreams were remembered was particularly high when the quality of sleep and creativity were at high levels, whereas the perception of stress, the frequency of waking during sleep, and the length of sleep were found to have no influence on the dreamer's ability to remember their dreams (Hill et al., 2007). "Good mood, good quality of sleep, female gender and creativity were clearly factors positively influencing the ability to remember dreams."

Case study

I should now like accompany these reflections on developmental psychology and neurobiology with some clinical observations drawn from a case study. The example is taken from a short-term psychoanalytical therapy which was carried out at the University of Leipzig Child Psychiatry Clinic.

The patient was a girl who recounted elaborate dreams—not always spontaneously, but quite often if asked. She also brought stories, fantasies, and daydreams into the therapy, and these were definitely of a similar nature to the accounts of her dreams.

It is probably no coincidence that this child, who was suffering from depressive symptoms, had shown herself to be a prolific storyteller in the story-telling test carried out before the start of her therapy. And in her stories she showed a marked degree of a quality termed intentionality in the theoretical system developed by Jonathan Hill (Hill et al., 2007). This is the ability to attribute underlying designs, intentions, and inner states to the protagonists of a story. Jonathon Hill saw this as a protective factor in boys against aggressive and hyperactive disorders. This ability was particularly marked in my patient and it made her an excellent story-teller. However, I sometimes had the feeling that this "putting herself rather too much in someone else's shoes" had its roots in anxiety, and strengthened rather than relieved the depressive mood. Was this an emphasis on others at the expense of self?

I will now go on to describe her treatment. Ulrike was eight years old and came to me for treatment over symptoms of depression. She had an aversion to school, was always getting into quarrels with school friends because she felt excluded, and she set her sights excessively high in her school work although she consistently had very good marks. She slept badly, waking often, and had an array of psychosomatic complaints that meant she frequently missed school. When she was going to stay the night with school friends she would ring up her mother and ask to be taken back home because she could not stand being there any longer.

She described a dream in the very first session. She had found a foreign baby on the street. It was a very dark-skinned child, but everything was somehow muddled up because it was really a boy she knew; it was Sven, from Scandinavia. Annabel, her particular enemy and a spoilsport in the class, said that the baby was *her* child or that it was her half-brother. But her friend Susanne said that this was not possible because Annabel's mother and step-father were not foreigners. So she had taken the baby to hospital because it had been injured, and there she had met her brother Kurt. Suddenly the baby had been sucked down the toilet and had disappeared. The residues of the day that she told me were: it was birthday, that Sven was the son of a family in Norway with whom they were friends, and that he was a boy who loved to play around toilets and with faeces and other excreta.

My associations were: the foreign baby is perhaps herself with a phantasy of being of unknown or foreign birth (cf., the Family Romance). I also noted regression to anal themes combined with phantasies of annihilation.

In the sixth session she started to draw straightaway, as if driven by an inner programme. She drew a locomotive with the engine driver sitting in it. The train was travelling on tracks over mountains. She said, "That's a railway track and there are mountains ahead." I remarked, "It takes a lot of power to get up the mountains." "That's why there's no carriage behind the engine. There's no-one else on the train except the engine driver," she explained. I asked, "Are you the engine driver who has to get over those high mountains? The engine driver is completely alone." She responded with, "If anything happens then someone comes to help. There's a competition between engines you see." And she drew a second locomotive further below. "But there's only one locomotive that manages to get over the mountain." She wrote "Miracle" on the side of the winning locomotive, and on the losing one she wrote "Katrin".

I commented that the losing locomotives, for example Katrin, might get jealous of the winner. She said, "The winner Miracle locomotive helps the others you know. The others could have managed but they were afraid. The Miracle locomotive was the only one who really set to work on the tasks," and I remarked, "When one is afraid, then one can't get over the mountain; one needs help." She drew balloons on the Miracle locomotive and stuck a balloon on a string on to it.

She then drew a second picture showing the Miracle locomotive with victor's laurels and a bow on it reading "1st place". She coloured in this locomotive with loving care in different colours. I commented "It seems to be a girl locomotive; it's being made to look particularly beautiful." "The locomotive doesn't care, actually," was the response.

"Oh, it just made me think of you and your brothers," I said. She answered, "I used to want be a princess and I had a princess costume but Konrad only liked the glamourous trousers, so after that I never put them on again."

Basically, in this dream-like narrative it is a question of the phallic little girl (or tomboy) who can tackle mountains particularly well and in the end becomes a strikingly beautiful, winning-locomotive-princess. It almost seems to be the exact opposite of the dark-skinned baby with his injuries. And opposite the winner is the ugly Katrin-locomotive, that cannot win anything. As if justifying her story, Ulrike said the winning locomotive could not help winning. After all, it was the only one who really tried. In this I see the possible rivalry with the mother object that, however, could potentially turn into what Katrin represents—a self-image of a black, injured, incapable locomotive, which is how Ulrike might sometimes feel, particularly in her depressions.

I commented, "These are perhaps the two sides in you, the one is a brightly coloured beautiful winner, but there is also the dark, maybe desperate, loser side." "I don't know." she said. And then she went on drawing and this time it was a box with various euro notes placed on it. She described how the audience had bet on the Miracle locomotive while the producers of the competition had favoured Katrin, and now the audience had won. She then put the picture on one side and seemed withdrawn. Any further talk about the pictures seemed out of the question. I nevertheless addressed her feelings in relation to the locomotives, saying that they might have something to do with her brothers. "My younger brother always gets in the way when I want to cuddle Mum. My older brother only gets at me because he's bored, cuddling Mum is the last thing he wants to do. He finds it all embarrassing—also when she cuddles Dad. My younger brother doesn't want to cuddle Dad so I have Dad all to myself."

In the eleventh session she drew the following picture. She started off strangely, drawing a figure with its face between its legs. At first I had the feeling it was a birth scene. In the end it became a cowboy sitting on a horse that had fallen over. Two Native Americans were drawn, seen from behind, but it was not clear if these were men or women. And then there was an Indian girl, with a doll, hiding behind a prickly cactus. Finally, it looked as though the fight between the cowboy and the Indians had been cancelled because the horse had slipped and fallen. She went on to explain that the cowboy was smiling in an embarrassed way because he had made a fool of himself, because the way he had fallen had injured the horse. The Indians were disappointed and worried because they still had the fight ahead of them. But the girl behind the cactus was relieved. She had been afraid because if they had lost the battle against the cowboy they would have had to leave their country. (Ulrike knows about the fate of the Indians) "And now," she said, "the girl could do something exciting that she would enjoy."

When we came to the associations she had with the picture, it was about the fights between boys in her class that she found frightening. She could also talk about the quarrels between her three brothers where she interfered, but where she was torn between being on the side of the younger ones or the elder ones. Most often she sided with the older boys. "Interfering in a fight is not so nice," she commented, and then she went on to describe in precise detail how the boys at school fought and the way this frightened her. The other girls interfered—could she do that, as a girl? Or did she have to hide behind the prickly cactus? Perhaps that is her basic dilemma: should she hide behind prickly cactuses or can she—as a girl—really enter into a relationship with others?

There were also quarrels between the grown-ups, she said, between Mum and her mother, and on one occasion this led to the grandmother leaving and going home. That had frightened everyone and had made them all sad. But her grandfather was more of a model for her. He kept out of it; he knew what his wife was like. It seems he diffused the tensions; he kept his distance as a non-involved third party. Ulrike was deeply involved in her drawing and in the discussion about her role as a girl in the fights between boys.

Fifteenth session

She told me about a dream. She was at a strange school and went home because she was ill. She lived round the corner from the school.

There was a girl there who was somehow her friend from her old class and she walked along with her. She thought it would not be noticed at school. At the door this friend's mother was waiting and came with them quickly. Suddenly, the friend turned into a little sister—which she does not have in real life (at first I did not notice this). They have to go over a hanging bridge. But she cannot get over because the bridge is hung the wrong way up—that is, it was a hanging bridge that swayed but with the planks above instead of underneath. She had to walk over this bridge every day. Her friend's mother said, "But that's much too dangerous particularly for the little sister".

Associations: she had been to a family gathering with her male cousin. Near the hotel they had wanted to go into a wood and then on into a meadow, but there was a river between the two and, apart from her elder brother, they had all got wet feet. That was when she had wished for a hanging bridge. The school (in the dream) was bewitched as if in a wood, like the one at the far end of Clara Park.

She then drew the dream. The friend's mother had strikingly large shoes. It was then that it occurred to me that the little sister in the dream was a wishful fantasy since she had only brothers. I pointed this out to her, and she said, "I do wish I had a little sister but there's no point because Mum and Dad don't want to have any more children. And besides, all that crying would get on my nerves. It's pointless. Little children are tiring." But she said, when I asked, that when she was grown-up she would like to have a baby, a little girl like Filina—the daughter of the family with whom they had been on holiday. She was so sweet. And she added that Daddy had also dreamed of having a little girl, called Martha—he had told her so. But she herself could do without all that crying. And also people had told her she would be put out because then Mummy would always have the baby on her arm. But she had not minded that at all, and she had not been jealous at all of her little brother. Quite the opposite: she had been very loving to him and had almost hugged him to death until they had told her to stop.

And anyway, she went on, she had talked to her father about dreams and they were always about wishes. But she had had nightmares that had had no wishes in them. For instance, there was the one with a bull that had pursued her, or the one in which she was going to be cooked. The bull dreams were about those bulls that were allowed to run around free in some countries—and they had blocked their way once. She was scared, she said. Actually she had had the dream before they had had the experience. But the bulls could wander around all over the place. It was alarming.

She mentioned another wish. She had wished to be a princess and had often dreamed about it.

I came back to the dream about being cooked. She said she had been in the garden with a little friend in the dream, and they had been deep in a game with the friend's mother. They had been called indoors, and suddenly the little friend disappeared. She, Ulrike, had run after her, and saw that she had gone over to a big party at the neighbours'. And then suddenly she had been locked up in the cellar by the mother of the neighbouring family and *she* had said: "I am going to cook you for supper." She had been terrified. She told me that sometimes she dreamt that she was sitting on the toilet and that then she soiled the bed. And it was a real nuisance that she had done that right up to starting school.

I asked her about the very big shoes the woman in her picture was wearing. It became clear that her friend's mother was rather strict and always hurrying them up because her daughter had to be in time for swimming practice.

At the end of this session she said that actually she was not so often afraid now; her symptoms were better. But in four weeks time, when they had to take blood for a test, she would be scared; that was unpleasant and made her afraid.

In my thoughts I find associations with the various dream segments. The wish to have children is ambivalent but in particular the instinctual drives connected with this (the hatred and aggression towards the little brother and the fantasised little sister but also possibly sexuality) are symbolised by the bull. Anxiety arises when these drives are not "held", are not fenced in, but roam free as in the open pastures of Norway. The mother in the picture perhaps symbolises the strict, revenge-seeking oedipal mother figure. But what can the curiously upside-down hanging bridge symbolise? Is there a reference here to sexuality? To danger? To crossing borders and rivers? Is there a connection here with her stomach pains: her own hunger but also the hunger of the mother who cooks children for supper? Everything appears to be ambivalent and have double references.

Conclusion

In the treatment of Ulrike there was a fluid transition from dream-like narrative that she created in the sessions to the narrative of her dreams. In the direct narratives it was a question of rivalries (the two locomotives, the cowboys and Indians). Were these the rivalries with her brothers? Or between her and her mother? In these narratives she managed to assert her interests (the winning locomotive, the Indian girl behind the prickly cactus) without a guilt-laden aggression turning against the self as was the mechanism in depression. The dreams show activities of infantile sexuality powered by instinctual drives: the oral voraciousness, projected on to the woman next door who plans to eat the children; the anal re-incorporation of the little injured child (into the mother?); and the phallic aggressive impulses represented by the bulls. The superego-like mother figures that crop up (the mother with the very large shoes) are neutralised.

But what could the strangely hung bridge represent? It is only clear that it is dangerous to go over it. Is this the path of development leading away from the mother? And Ulrike sees she cannot go along it? This bridge offers nothing to hold on to. Is this a symbol for the lack of support she had experienced in her development?

And where is our analytic work in all this? Is it also represented in the dreams? For analysis had offered a vessel into which the dream stories, and also the dream-like narratives, could be safely deposited. It was at any rate clear to Ulrike that the dreams expressed parts of her psychical reality, and that exchanging ideas about them was a healing process in her development.

References

Aserinsky, E., & Kleitman, N. (1953). Regularly occurring periods of eye motility, and concomitant phenomena, during sleep. *Science*, *118*(3062): 273–274.

Brand, S., Beck, J., Kalak, N., Gerber, M., Kirov, R., Puhse, U., & Holsboer-Trachsler, E. (2011). Dream recall and its relationship to sleep, perceived stress, and creativity among adolescents. *Journal of Adolescent Health*, *49*(5): 525–531.

Hill, J., Fonagy, P., Lancaster, G., & Broyden, N. (2007). Aggression and intentionality in narrative responses to conflict and distress story stems: an investigation of boys with disruptive behaviour problems. *Attachment and Human Development, 9*(3): 223–237.

Hobson, J. A. (2009). REM sleep and dreaming: towards a theory of protoconsciousness. *Nature Reviews Neuroscience, 10*(11): 803–813.

Kaplan-Solms, K. S., & Solms, M. (2000). *Clinical Studies in Neuro-Psychoanalysis*. London: Karnac.

Koukkou, M., & Lehmann, D. (2000). Traum und Hirnforschung. In: B. Boothe, (Ed.). *Der Traum—hundert Jahre nach Freuds Traumdeutung* (pp. 227–249). Zürich: vdf.

Solms, M. (2011). Neurobiology and the neurological basis of dreaming. *Handbook of Clinical Neurology, 98*: 519–544.

Solms, M., & Lechevalier, B. (2002). Neurosciences and psychoanalysis. *International Journal of Psychoanalysis, 83*(1): 233–237.

INDEX

affect(ive), xiv, 23, 26, 29–30, 72–74, 76, 78, 90, 107
   agitated, 107
   arousal, 114
   associated, xiv
   interaction, 29–30
   reversed, 19
   state, 27
aggression, 1–2, 5, 7–8, 19, 25, 29, 50, 57, 79, 82–83, 88–89, 116, 121
   drive, 18
   fantasy, 88
   feelings, 18
   guilt-laden, 122
   impulse, 1, 8, 122
   symptoms, 18
   tensions, 18
   thoughts, 75
   wild, 87
anxiety, 1, 23, 25–27, 29, 31–32, 35, 41, 45, 55, 57–58, 61, 63, 65–66, 116, 121
   acute, 36
   castration, xiii, 1, 3–6, 11–12, 14, 29, 34–35, 37, 47
   death, 45
   depression, 103
   dream, xiii, 3–6, 8, 15–16, 20, 24–26, 28–29, 36, 61, 76
   object loss, 3
   primitive, 56
   retaliation, 14
Anzieu, A., 40
Anzieu, D., 55
Aserinsky, E., 111

attention, xii, 36, 42, 51, 58, 60
   capacity of, 42–43
   competencies, 43
   spontaneous, 42
   to dreams, xi, 18

Beck, J., 115
Benjamin, W., xv
Blechterev, V., 98
Bion, W. R., xi, 40–42, 48, 50–51, 55–57, 59, 65, 94, 101
Bornstein, B., 5, 14
Brand, S., 115
Broyden, N., 115–116

case studies *see also*: clinical examples
   Anja, 93, 96–98, 102–103, 105–108
   Christine, 18–19
   Johnny, xiii, 6–8, 30–37, 72–75
   Kevin, 87–89
   Little Hans, xiii, 6, 8–9, 26–27, 29, 34, 37
   Mark, 79–86
   Max, 1–2
   Peter, 56–65
   Ulrike, 116–122
clinical examples *see also*: case studies
   Chapter Three
      Example One, 40–41
      Example Two, 43–44
      Example Three, 45
      Example Four (*Paul*), 45–48
      Example Five, 48–49
      Example Six, 49

Example Seven, 49–50
Example Eight, 50
conscious(ness), 29, 44, 47, 57, 77, 95–97, 104–105, 107–108, 112, 115
    see also: unconscious(ness)
    conflicts, 31
    development of, 112
    dream, 112
    perception, 115
    pre-, 43, 47, 56, 63, 94–97, 100–101, 104–107
    preoccupation, 75
    proto-, 111–112
    rudimentary, 57
    secondary, 112
    sub-, xii
    thinking, 89
    waking, 111
    wishes, 23
containment, xii, 24, 26, 41–42, 49, 51, 55–57, 59, 62–66, 94, 103, 108
countertransference, 16–17, 25, 56, 108
    see also: transference

depression, 24, 49, 56, 58, 116, 118, 122
    see also: anxiety
Diatkine, R., 51
disorder
    hyperactive, 116
    language development, 79
    major, 37
    sleep, 3–5, 15, 18, 24, 58–59

ego, 11, 15, 18–19, 26, 29, 64–65, 95
    achievement of, 19
    age-appropriate, 11
    boundaries, 63
    child's, 3
    defence, 36–37
    development, xiii, 2–5, 9–10, 12, 15, 20, 31, 49, 71, 75
    differentiation, 65
    evolving, 26
    function, 4, 6, 9, 12, 23, 25, 65, 76
    immature, 64
    -regression, 16
    resistances, 52
    stronger, 63
    structures, 11
    super, 2–3, 10–11, 15, 29, 34, 37, 71, 122
    weakened, 19
elements, 42, 45, 50, 72, 75, 85, 88, 99, 106
    see also: unconscious(ness)
    beta, xi, 59, 73, 76, 90, 103, 107

concrete, 59
of distortion, 12
of dream-work, 8, 19
repeated, 33
sensorial, 42
thinkable, 55
traumatic, 7
visual, 10
Ellman, S. J., 90

Fain, M., 65
fantasy, xii–xiii, 10–11, 13–14, 17, 20, 26, 45, 55–56, 64, 76–79, 89, 113, 116, 121
    see also: aggression, life, unconscious(ness)
    activity, 51
    animals, 82–83
    destructive, 83
    of omnipotence, 2
    of seduction, 47
    primal, 46
    verbal, xiii, 50
    wishful, 78, 120
Fenichel, O., 14–15
Ferenczi, S., 56, 64
Ferro, A., 103
Fischmann, T., 90
Fonagy, P., 79, 107, 115–116
Fraiberg, S., 4–5, 14
free association, 5–6, 9, 16–18, 37, 70–71
Freud, A., xii–xiii, 3, 5–6, 12, 20, 30, 40
Freud, S., xi–xiv, 3, 6–7, 9–10, 13, 15, 26–30, 39–43, 47, 51, 63, 69–71, 75–78, 93–101, 104, 106–108

Gerber, M., 115
Gergely, G., 79, 107
Grotjahn, M., 17, 72
Guignard, F., 41, 44
guilt, 5, 10, 18, 34, 63, 75, 122
Gunter, M., 90

hallucination, 51, 66
    drive fulfilment, 3
    experience, 70
    quality, 77
    realisation, 39
    satisfaction, 3, 51
Hau, S., 90
Hill, J., 115–116
Hobson, J. A., 111–114
Hoffer, W., 14
Holsboer-Trachsler, E., 115
Hopf, H., 11